THE CZECH
REPUBLIC

THE CZECH

REPUBLIC

STEVEN OTFINOSKI

* Facts On File, Inc.

The Czech Republic

Facts On File, Inc.
11 Penn Plaza
New York NY 10001

Library of Congress Cataloging-in-Publication Data

Otfinoski, Steven.
    The Czech Republic / by Steven Otfinoski.
      p. cm. — (Nations in transition)
    Includes bibliographical references and index.
Summary: Chronicles the history of the Czech Republic and explores daily life, politics, and the many challenges facing the country since the decline of Communism and the emergence of democracy.
    ISBN 0–8160–3080–4 (hb : alk. paper)
    1. Czech Republic—Juvenile literature. [1. Czech Republic.]
I. Title. II. Series.
DB2011.087 1996
943.7'03—dc20
                                           95–3270 6

Fact On File books are available at special discounts when purchased in bulk quantities for businesses, associations, institutions or sales promotions. Please call our Special Sales Department in New York at 212/967-8800 or 800/322-8755.

Text design by Catherine Rincon Hyman
Cover design by Nora Wertz
Map Illustrations by Dale Williams

MP FOF 10 9 8 7 6 5 4 3 2 1

This book is printed on acid-free paper.

Printed in the United States of America

Contents

1

An Introduction to the Land and Its People

---

*T*he Czech Republic, established on January 1, 1993, is one of the newest nations in Eastern Europe. However, the land and its nation are centuries old. In a part of Europe that has seen change and strife throughout its long history, the Czechs have endured their share of upheaval.

When talking about the Czech land, *lands* is the more appropriate word. Three distinct regions developed here in the center of Europe, sharing a common language, culture and ethnic background—Bohemia, Moravia and Silesia.

An independent part of the Holy Roman Empire, the Czech lands were later subjugated by the Austrian Empire for three centuries. Then in 1918, following World War I, the Czechs and their neighbors, the Slovaks, joined to form a new and independent nation, Czechoslovakia. It was to become one of the most democratic nations in Eastern Europe during the next 20 years. Czechoslovakia survived both the Nazi occupation of World War II and the more than 40-year reign of the Communists following that war, but it could not survive either freedom in 1990 or internal turmoil between the Czechs and Slovaks—two peoples closely joined by blood but separated by their political and economic past.

Throughout all these changes, the Czechs have retained their ingenuity, their industry and their imagination. Inhabitants of one of the most highly industrialized nations in Eastern Europe with a standard of living that is the envy of its neighbors, the Czechs have always balanced materialism with intellectual concerns. Their national heroes are innovators and rugged individualists—Jan Hus, the rebel priest who defied the pope and prefigured the Protestant Reformation by more than a century; Franz Kafka, the quiet Jewish writer whose bizarre, metaphorical stories and novels ushered in the psychological literature expressive of the 20th century's anxiety and alienation; Alexander Dubcek, the courageous Communist leader who for a brief time gave socialism "a human face"; and Václav Havel, the playwright who became his country's number-one dissenter against the Communists and the new republic's first head of state. Where else but in the Czech Republic could a playwright become president of his country?

The Czech people are individualists, as American writer Patricia Hampl discovered while riding a streetcar in Prague, the capital city:

> The tram was crowded, as trams in Prague usually are. I had to stand at the back, wedged in with a lot of other people. . . . Then I saw, very near to me, the falconer and his bird. A man, dressed in green like a true man of the forest in knee pants with high leather boots and a green leather short jacket. On his head he wore a cap of soft velvet, possibly suede, with a feather on the side. But most incredible was the falcon that clove to his gloved hand with its lacquered claws, its head covered with a tiny leather mask topped, as the hunter's own cap was, with a small, stiff plume. . . . The falconer seemed perfectly at ease in the back of the crowded car, when he got off, at the Slavia

stop, next to the National Theater, and stood waiting for a connecting tram, it was the rest of the world and not he that looked inappropriate. . . . They struck me as emblems of the nation.

At the Crossroads of Europe

The Czech Republic is one of the smallest countries in Eastern Europe, consisting of 30,449 square miles (78,864 sq km). Poland, one of its nearest neighbors, is four times the size of the Czech Republic. Only Slovakia and Albania are smaller. The country's population is 10,408,000 (1992 estimate). About 94 percent of the people are ethnic Czechs, and about

The almost ethereal beauty and enchantment of the Czech Republic is typified by Prague, its capital, seen here at dusk. Hradcany Castle, also known as Prague Castle, looms over the centuries-old city. The Vltava River flows in the foreground.
(Tony Savino/Impact Visuals)

3 percent are Slovak. The remaining fraction of the population is made up of Hungarians, Poles, Germans, Ukrainians and Gypsies. Nearly three-quarters of the people live in urban areas.

Completely landlocked, the Czech Republic is bordered on the north by Poland and Germany, on the south by Austria, on the southeast and east by Slovakia and on the northwest and west by Germany. In the center of Central Europe, the Czech lands have often been called the "crossroads of Europe," which helps explain historically their importance as a place where both goods and ideas are exchanged.

Bohemia

Geographically, the Czech Republic is divided into three regions, each with its own past and traditions—Bohemia, Moravia and Silesia. Bohemia is the largest and westernmost part of the country. It is basically a flat plateau surrounded by mountains and forests. The Bohemian Mountains, which are comprised of the Ore Mountains on the northwest German border and the Bohemian Forest to the southwest, are actually large hills rising about 2,500 feet (762 m) above sea level. The Ore Mountains are rich in coal and uranium ore, while the Bohemian Forest produces lumber and other wood products. Fertile soil covers the mountains, making them perfect for raising crops and livestock. They also draw thousands of Czechs and foreign tourists each year to their ski resorts and health spas.

To the northeast lie the Sudetic Mountains, which border Poland and are more rugged and higher than the Bohemian Mountains. The highest peak in the Czech Republic, Snezka (5,256 feet, 1,602.5 m), is found here. The mountains are home to a number of important industrial cities and towns. The Bohemian-Moravian Highlands are on the west and extend through a good part of southern Bohemia into southwestern Moravia. Most of the region is farmland, although Pilsen (Plzen in Czech), its largest city, is well known for its many breweries. The Bohemian Basin, the heart of the region, has farmland that is irrigated by the country's two major rivers—the Vltava (Moldau), flowing northward and the Elbe, flowing westward. Prague, the country's capital and largest city, lies along the Vltava in north-central Bohemia.

For centuries, Czech poets, composers and artists have praised the natural beauty of the Bohemian rivers and woodlands, perhaps none more eloquently than composer Bedrich Smetana (1824–1884), the father of Czech classical music. In "The Moldau," one part of his six-movement epic symphonic poem *Ma Vlast* (*My Fatherland*) (1874–79), Smetana recreated the river's progress in sound. Here is an excerpt from the written preface to the score:

> Two springs pour forth their streams in the shade of the Bohemian forest, the one warm and gushing, the other cold and tranquil. Their waves, joyfully flowing over their rocky beds, unite and sparkle in the morning sun. The first brook, rushing on, becomes the River Moldau, which with its waters speeding through Bohemia's valleys, grows into a mighty stream. . . . At the Rapids of St. John the stream speeds on, winding its way through cataracts and hewing the path for its foaming waters through the rocky chasm into the broad river-bed in which it flows on in majestic calm toward Prague. . . .

Moravia

To the east of Bohemia is Moravia, a region of lowlands that is home to industry and mining. Brno, in the southwest, is the country's second-largest city and one of Europe's largest textile centers. While Bohemia is larger and more historically celebrated, Moravians have their own regional pride, as writer Hampl learned during a brief stopover in Brno:

> Moravia is distinguished from Brno by a more elusive cultural quality. Moravians think of themselves as the *real* Czechs. Joseph Wechsberg, a Moravian himself, says the attitude of Moravians toward the rest of the Czechs is rather like that of a Boston Yankee to the West. . . . As we passed by a scaffolded old building, she [a Czech friend] pointed and said, "Older than Prague."

The Morava River, the easternmost part of Moravia, forms a fertile valley where many crops are grown. Still further to the northeast is Ostrava, an industrial center where coal is mined and iron and steel are produced.

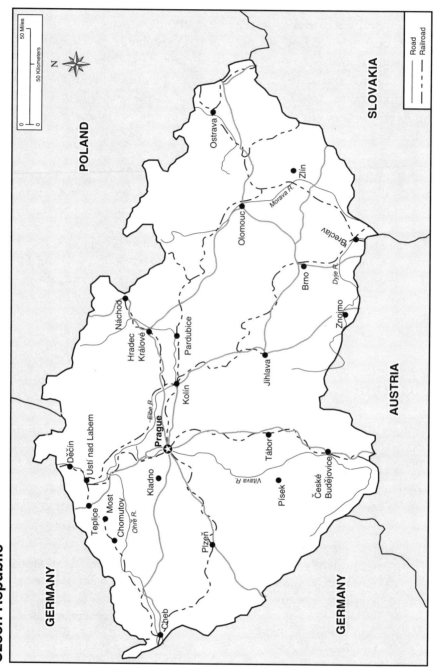

Czech Republic

Silesia

The third historical region, tiny Silesia, straddles the Czech Republic and Poland. Czech Silesia, the smaller of the two sections, contains the Karviná basin, a rich source of coal. The black smoke that rises from its coal-fueled factories has given it the name the Black Country. The northern section of Silesia is comprised of wooded but fertile lowland used for farming vegetables.

Climate

The climate of the Czech Republic is somewhere between maritime and continental, with mildly cold winters and warm summers. Average temperatures range from 29°F (-2°C) in January to 66°F (19°C) in July. The average annual precipitation is 28 inches (71 cm).

The Czech Republic is a lovely land of rolling hills, pleasant farms and historic but bustling cities. The Czechs are justifiably proud of their well-crafted goods, their fine crops, and their world-famous beer. They are also proud of the restless, creative minds that produced model nation-states and great works of literature, music and cinema. A practical people with a rich imagination, their often-troubled history has put both these sides of their national character to the supreme test.

NOTES

p. 2   "The tram was crowded . . . " Patricia Hampl, *A Romantic Education* (Boston: Houghton Mifflin, 1981), pp. 208–09.

p. 5   "Two springs pour forth . . . " Liner notes, recording of Bedrich Smetana's "The Moldau," performed by the Cleveland Orchestra, CBS's Great Performances series.

p. 5   "Moravia is distinguished from Brno . . . " Patricia Hampl, *A Romantic Education*, p. 257.

2

From a Medieval Kingdom to a Modern Nation-State (Prehistory to 1918)

*M*ore than 2,500 years ago, the Czech people lived on the plains of Central Asia and what is now Russia with their fellow Slavs, the Slovaks. They were a hard-working and peaceful people, preferring farming and raising livestock to warfare. This made them an attractive target for a barbaric tribe from the East, the Avars. These Mongolian invaders drove the Czechs and Slovaks westward in about A.D. 500, enslaving them in the region of Central Europe that they inhabit to this day.

Under the strong leadership of their tribal chief Samo, the Slavs rose up against the Avars in 620 and defeated them. Determined to keep their freedom, the Czechs and Slovaks built permanent settlements of wood and stone with strong defense points. About a century later, two Greek missionaries, saints Cyril (A.D. c. 827–869) and Methodius (A.D. c. 825–884), arrived in the Czech lands and brought Christianity to these pagan people. They also taught them a new alphabet, later known as Cyrillic, after Cyril, who developed it from the Greek alphabet.

By 800, the Czechs and Slovaks had joined other Slavic tribes to form the Great Moravian Empire, which encompassed much of Central Europe. But the empire was short-lived. The Magyars, fierce warriors from neighboring Hungary, invaded their land and destroyed the empire. They

Three of the Premyslide kings—the first rulers of Bohemia—are pictured in this late 14th-century pen drawing. From the left they are Otakar II, Wenceslas II and Wenceslas III, the last of the dynasty, who died in 1306. The line was founded by the legendary Queen Libussa and her peasant husband Premysl. (The New York Public Library Picture Collection)

took over Slovakia, making the Slovaks their vassals for the next thousand years. The more-fortunate Czechs, however, escaped Hungarian domination and went on to found their own kingdom.

The Rise of Bohemia

About A.D. 900, Queen Libussa and her consort, the peasant Premysl, founded the first Czech royal dynasty. The Romans, who had invaded the area centuries earlier, had named it Boiohaemia, after a Celtic tribe, the Boii, who were driven out by the

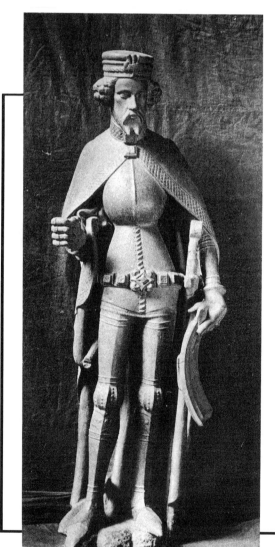

King Charles IV (1316–78)

If any one person was responsible for the golden age of Bohemia, it was Charles IV, king of Germany, Bohemia and eventually Holy Roman Emperor.

He was born in Prague, the city he would one day make great, the eldest son of John of Luxembourg, king of Bohemia. At age eight, as was the cus-

Charles IV, one of the great kings of Bohemia, ushered in its golden age in the 14th century. His legacy is evident today in the palaces, churches and monuments of Prague.
(The Bettmann Archive)

Czechs when they first entered the region. For the next four centuries, the Premysl kings ruled over the kingdom of Bohemia.

The first great historical Bohemian ruler was Wenceslas (c. 907–929), a Bohemian prince whose piety is celebrated in the still-popular Christmas carol that bears his name. Wenceslas worked hard to establish Christianity in Bohemia and forged an alliance with his former enemy, Henry I of Germany. Under Wenceslas, Bohemia and Moravia were united under a single crown, but his allegiance to Christianity earned him the hatred of the nobility, who were supported by Wenceslas's brother, aptly named Boleslav the Cruel (d. 967). In 929, Boleslav assassinated Wenceslas as the latter was going to church; then he seized the throne—his major aim—and further promoted Christianity. By the next century, Wenceslas (Václav in Czech) was recognized as the patron saint of Bohemia.

---

tom among royalty, Charles was married to Blanche, sister of Philip IV of France. His close friendship with Pope Clement VI, who helped him become king of Germany in 1346, earned him the nickname "the priests' king."

When his father died a month later defending France from the English at the Battle of Crécy, Charles became king of Bohemia. In 1354 he crossed the Alps to reach Rome, where he was crowned Holy Roman Emperor. Prague was now the capital of the empire, and Charles saw that the city looked the part. He rebuilt the Cathedral of St. Vitus in the lighter, more luminous French style, constructed castles that seemed to soar, laid out the neat streets of Prague's New Town and founded Charles University in 1348, the oldest university in Central Europe.

Charles was an enthusiastic patron of the arts and entertained the Italian poet Petrarch and other writers and intellectuals in Prague. Fluent in five languages, he helped the development of the written German language. His Golden Bull*, issued in 1356, made the state secure from papal interference by entrusting the selection of future emperors to seven electors. It also assured the kingdom of Bohemia the right of self-government within the empire. This bull would remain in force until the downfall of the Holy Roman Empire in 1806.

A strong and wise monarch, Charles secured the succession for his eldest son, Wenceslas, before his death. He was buried in St. Vitus's Cathedral, one of the many monuments that he left the people of Prague.

* A bull is a decree handed down by a sovereign or other person in authority.

Boleslav soon found himself at the mercy of the German king Otto I, who incorporated Bohemia into his Holy Roman Empire*. Although a part of the empire, Bohemia largely retained its right to self-government.

The next great Bohemian king was Charles IV (see boxed biography), who succeeded his father, the blind but valiant King John (1296–46), killed at the battle of Crécy in France, while fighting against the English. Charles quickly proved an outstanding state builder. In his 30-year reign, he made Bohemia one of the greatest kingdoms in medieval Europe. Many of the fine churches and other structures Charles had built, such as the Cathedral of St. Vitus and Charles Bridge, the only bridge to span the Vltava River until the 19th century, still stand today. His greatest achievement was Charles University in Prague, founded in 1348, the first institution of higher learning in Central Europe. In 1355, Charles was crowned Holy Roman Emperor and made Prague the capital of his empire.

Religious Reform and the Hussite Movement

But the Golden Age of Bohemia would be quickly followed by a time of darkness and division. As one historian has wryly observed, the Holy Roman Empire was not holy, was not Roman and was not an empire. The Roman Catholic Church shared the power of the state with royalty, and high church officials abused their privilege at the people's expense. In Prague, a priest, Jan Hus (see boxed biography), dared to speak out against the corruption of the church and called for a movement back to the simple teachings of Christ as set down in the Bible. The fact that Hus preached to the people not in German, the established language of the church and state, but in his native Czech, made him an even greater threat to the upper classes. Thus, Hus's religious rebellion was also a social and nationalistic one. As rector of the University of Prague, Hus gathered a faithful following in the city and surrounding areas until he was excommunicated by the pope for his outspokenness in 1411. The Germans tricked him into coming to the Council of Constance in Germany in 1414

---

* A Christian state, centered in Germany, that claimed to continue the tradition of the fallen Roman Empire.

to explain his actions. Once there, he was arrested, tried and condemned as a heretic. In July 1415, Jan Hus was burned at the stake for defying the power of the church.

Hus's death made him a martyr to his followers, called Hussites. For the next two decades, the Hussites, anti-Catholic Bohemian nationalists, fought against the Catholic Holy Roman Empire in the Hussite Wars. The conflict finally ended in 1436 in compromise, allowing the Hussites some freedom of worship, but by then, many of them had fled Bohemia and were living as wandering exiles in Europe. They gave a new meaning to the word *Bohemian,* which is still used to describe a person who lives an unconventional lifestyle. Many of these Bohemians later settled in the United States, where they finally found the religious freedom they had been searching for. However, the corruption they had fought against continued to grow and infect every part of the Bohemian state.

Czech nobles, anxious to retain their own power, brought in foreign kings from Poland whom they could control. Weak and divided, Bohemia finally fell prey to neighboring Austria, ruled, as the Holy Roman Empire was, by one of Europe's most powerful dynasties—the Hapsburgs.

Revolt and Defeat

In 1526, Hapsburg emperor Ferdinand I (1503–64) became ruler over Bohemia, although the kingdom retained some of its independence. About the same time the Protestant Reformation, led by Martin Luther in Germany, swept across Europe. Many Czechs, longing to be freed from the Catholic Hapsburgs, became Protestants. The emperor sent in priests belonging to the Society of Jesus (Jesuits), a scholarly religious order founded in 1534 by Saint Ignatius Loyola, to restore Catholicism to heretic Bohemia. When Ferdinand's descendant, Emperor Matthias, refused to grant them religious freedom, members of the Bohemian parliament threw two of his councilors out the window of Prague's Hradcany Castle in May 1618. This was an old Bohemian punishment for unjust or corrupt officials.

The incident sparked The Thirty Years' War, a religious conflict between Protestants and Roman Catholics. From Bohemia, the war spread to Protestant Denmark and Sweden, who opposed the Catholic German states. In its last phase, the war became a purely political struggle between

Jan Hus
(1372–1415)

The Protestant Reformation of the 16th century was anticipated more than one hundred years earlier by this greatest of Czech religious reformers.

John Hus was born in southwest Bohemia in the village of Husince. He was known as "John of Husince" and later dropped all but the first three letters of the village's name. Although a peasant by birth, Hus had a brilliant mind and was accepted into the University of Prague in 1390. Ten years later he was ordained a priest in the Roman Catholic Church and made dean of the faculty the following year.

Religious reformer Jan Hus awaits his execution in a German prison in this painting by Josef Mathauser. Although he died in 1415, Hus's reforms would change the course of Bohemia's history for centuries to come.
(The New York Public Library Picture Collection)

the Bourbon dynasty of France and the Hapsburgs, who ruled Germany and Austria. The army of Emperor Matthias decisively defeated the Czech nobles at the Battle of the White Mountain in 1620. The proud kingdom of Bohemia was reduced to a fiefdom of the Hapsburgs. The kingdom was divided into three parts—Bohemia, Moravia and Silesia. The cultural heritage of the Czechs was wiped out as the zealous Jesuits burned whole libraries of precious books containing the glory of Czech literature. The Czechs were forced to give up their language and to speak and write in

The clergy in Bohemia, who owned about half of all the land in the country, frequently abused their power. Hus, under the influence of the great English reformer John Wycliffe (c. 1330–84), attacked the church leaders, calling the papacy an "institution of Satan." A strong nationalist, Hus preached publicly in Czech, when most clerics spoke in the dominant German language.

Although accused by church leaders of heresy, Hus had powerful protectors in the archbishop of Prague and King Wenceslas IV of Bohemia. In 1409 he was appointed rector of the University but was excommunicated in 1412 by the church for his fiery preaching against clerical abuse.

In 1412, King Sigismund of Germany, Wenceslas's half brother, persuaded Hus to come to Germany to argue his case in Constance. Hus agreed but soon found he had been tricked into leaving the safety of Prague. He was arrested upon his arrival and put in prison. During three public hearings, Hus defended himself convincingly. Given the chance to recant his teachings, he refused and was sentenced to death. He was burned at the stake, the common sentence for heretics, on July 6, 1415. Made a national hero by his death, Hus was later declared a martyr to his faith by the University of Prague. His reforms lived on in his followers who called themselves Hussites and later divided into two groups—conservatives and radicals. The conservatives made a peaceful treaty with the Catholic Church in 1433 and were granted the right to worship. The radicals fought the church and were defeated the following year. In 1457, some Hussites formed the Unity of Brethren, based on Hus's teachings, and later became the Moravian Church. The Moravian Church still flourishes today in the Czech Republic, other European countries and the United States.

German. Roman Catholicism became the state religion, and Czech culture and traditions were cruelly suppressed. The Hapsburgs, however, could not wrench the idea of their nation from the hearts of the people.

The 19th-Century Nationalist Movement

Their national identity ruthlessly repressed, the Czechs found other channels for their energies. The Industrial Revolution that swept England in the late 18th century erupted in Bohemia and Moravia. While their neighbors in Eastern Europe were still living in a basically agricultural society as they had for centuries, the Czechs were developing factories and other industrial works at an incredible rate. Peasants from the countryside swarmed into the cities to work in these new factories and businesses. Cities such as Prague and Brno developed into centers of intellectualism as well as industry; out of this intellectual ferment arose a new spirit of Slavic pride and Czech nationalism. The leading light of this Pan-Slavic movement was writer and historian Frantisek Palacký (1798–1876). In his monumental *History of the Czech Nation* (1836–67), Palacký viewed the history of his people as an ongoing struggle between the Slavs and the Germans that would end in the reemergence of the Czech lands as a free and independent republic. He did not advocate a violent revolution to accomplish this, but he fostered self-affirmation through education.

Although nonviolent, Palacký was steadfast in his nationalism. When invited in 1848 by the German congress in Frankfurt to hold elections in his homeland for representatives to a constitutional convention meant to establish a new federation of German states, he wrote back

> I am not a German. . . . I am a Czech of Slavonic blood. . . . That nation is a small one, it is true, but from time immemorial it has been a nation by itself and depends upon its own strength. Its rulers were from ancient times members of the federation of German princes, but the nation never regarded itself as belonging to the German nation, nor throughout all these centuries has it been regarded by others as so belonging. . . . I must briefly express my conviction that those who ask that Austria and with her Bohemia should unite on national lines with Germany, are demanding that she should commit suicide—a step lacking either moral or political sense. . . .

Palacký died in 1876, never seeing his dream of a Czech republic fulfilled. However, he inspired young men such as Tomás Masaryk (see boxed biography, Chapter 3) and Edvard Benes (1884–1948), both of whom would help transform that dream into reality.

In 1867, the Hapsburgs's Austrian Empire joined with Hungary to form the Austro-Hungarian Empire. After a thousand years of separation, fate had joined the Czechs and Slovaks together once again. This time they would suffer jointly as subjects of the same tyrannical master. Increased taxation and economic misery turned the national movement more radical, with more and more Czech reformers calling for complete separation from the Austrians and the Hungarians as the only solution.

In 1914 World War I broke out. The Austro-Hungarian Empire sided with the Germans against England, France and (after 1917) the United States. Czechs and Slovaks were drafted to fight, but many deserted rather than help their despised masters win the war. As the conflict wore on, revolutionary ferment increased in the Czech lands. Many nationalist leaders were arrested, but Masaryk and Benes escaped and fled to France. In Paris in 1916, they helped found the Czechoslovak national council, an organization dedicated to gaining support from the Allies for an independent, democratic state for their peoples.

The war ended in German defeat and the complete dismantling of the Austro-Hungarian Empire; freedom was granted to Bohemia, Moravia and Silesia. But Masaryk knew that to survive in a new Europe, the old Slavic tribes of Czechs and Slovaks would have to join together. So in 1919, at the Treaty of Versailles, with the full support of the United States and its allies, a new nation was born—the republic of Czechoslovakia.

NOTES

p. 16 "I am not a German. . . . " S. Harrison Thomson, *Czechoslovakia in European History* (Princeton, N.J.: Princeton University Press, 1943), pp. 45–46.

3

Czechoslovakia Under Two Brutal Masters (1918–1985)

*T*he new nation of Czechoslovakia was only one of a number of new and independent countries to rise out of the ashes of World War I—the others included Poland, Hungary and Yugoslavia—but none got off to a more promising start. Tomás Masaryk was elected the country's first president and he worked effectively to make Czechoslovakia a model of capitalist democracy. A new constitution was drawn up and implemented and industry grew and expanded.

But there were serious problems to be faced. The economy was in flux, unemployment was rampant and ethnic unrest was on the rise. The

Out of the ashes of World War I, Czechoslovakia arose as a new and independent republic. Here, its first president, Tomás Masaryk, is cheered by the people of Prague as he parades through the streets of the new capital. (The Bettmann Archive)

Czechs made up only 51 percent of the population, but they controlled the government. The Slovaks, poorer and less urbanized than the Czechs, were justifiably upset. To worsen the situation, 3½ million Germans living in the Sudetic Mountains area known as Sudetenland were clamoring for their own rights. For all his good intentions, Masaryk did little to alleviate the ethnic unrest, and by the 1930s the division between the Czechs and the rest of the populace was a serious one.

In 1935, after 16 years in power, Tomás Masaryk resigned as president. His longtime colleague Edvard Benes succeeded him. Benes did his best to continue Masaryk's policies, but Europe had become a more troubled place than it had been in 1918. In Germany, Adolf Hitler (1889–1945) had come to power and promised to restore Germany to its former glory before the humiliating defeat of World War I. Part of that glory rested on conquering new lands and subjecting their peoples to German imperialism.

The Nazi Occupation and World War II

In March 1938, Hitler's troops marched into Austria, his nation's former ally, and were greeted in the streets as liberators. Next, Hitler turned his attention to the Sudetenland of Czechoslovakia. Hitler warned the Czechs that unless they granted self-rule to the Sudeten Germans, he would declare war. In September 1938, Prime Minister Neville Chamberlain (1869–1940) of Great Britain and French premier Édouard Daladier (1884–1970) met in Munich, Germany, with Hitler and his ally, Benito Mussolini (1883–1945), Italy's Fascist leader. The Czechs were not invited to attend. Hitler assured the other leaders that he would make no further

Three women in the town of Eger salute arriving German troops in 1938 in this powerful photograph. Their reactions symbolize the different responses of the Czechs to the Nazi occupation of their country—jubilation, resignation and devastation. The Nazis stayed for six and one-half years. (The Bettmann Archive)

territorial claims in Europe if they allowed him to take the Sudetenland. Chamberlain and Daladier, anxious to avoid war, agreed not to interfere, although both had previously supported Czechoslovakia. Chamberlain returned to Great Britain from the Munich Pact proclaiming he had helped make "peace for our time."

But in Czechoslovakia, the time for peace had ended. Unable to resist Hitler's Nazi troops, the Czechs reluctantly seceded the Sudetenland to him in 1938. With this occurrence, President Benes and the legitimate democratic government had fled the country and set up a government-in-exile in London.

In early 1939, Hitler's troops marched into Prague and made the entire country a German "protectorate." None of Czechoslovakia's allies came to its defense. When Hitler invaded Poland a few months later, the West realized, too late, that the German dictator was bent on dominating all of Europe. Two days later, England and France declared war on Germany, and World War II was under way.

The Soviet Union, a Communist dictatorship, offered to help Czechoslovakia if the Western allies followed suit; the democratic Czech government-in-exile gave full support to the Western powers and the Soviet Union. The Czech and Slovak Communist Party therefore helped the war resistance within the country during the long German occupation. These two actions made the Czechs look more sympathetically on the Communists than on the Western powers.

One of the first countries to come under Nazi control in the war, Czechoslovakia escaped the wholesale destruction that befell many of its neighbors in Eastern Europe, but the Czechs did not survive the war unscathed. When Nazi governor of Prague Reinhard Heydrich was assassinated in 1942, the Nazis exacted a brutal revenge: the entire adult male populations of the Czech towns of Lidice and Lezaky were executed, the women were sent to concentration camps and the children sent to their deaths in mobile gas chambers.

Frantisek Kraus, a concentration-camp survivor, was part of a work gang assigned to dig mass graves at Lidice during the slaughter. Here is how he remembers the grim event in his book *Art from the Ashes*:

> The air rages like a wounded cyclop and hurtles the deadly rocks down to us again. Bricks drop onto the empty church benches, jump high again and dance to and fro as if it were a festive church holiday,

then the beams clatter down and break the roof, walls and vaultings shake, pictures of saints in gold frames fall from the old walls, and thunder to the ground.

When the Slovak Communist Party staged an uprising in August 1944, it was ruthlessly put down by the Nazis. By the war's end, 360,000 Czechs and Slovaks had died.

But the Germans had taken on too many enemies and ultimately lost the war. In early 1945, Czechoslovakia was liberated by Soviet troops from the east and U.S. troops from the west.

The Communists Take Over

Benes returned to set up a new government, but he found himself taking on a new unwelcome partner in power—the Communists. Many Czechs, however, were grateful to the Communists, who had stood by them in resisting the Nazis. They praised the Communist plan to appropriate land from the 3 million deported Sudeten Germans and redistribute it to Czech and Slovak peasants.

In the election of 1946, the Communist Party won 38 percent of the vote. Benes, reelected president, formed a new coalition government—the National Front—with the Communists. Communist Party leader Klement Gottwald (1896–1953) was named premier. About half of the government ministers were Communists and half non-Communist. One of the most influential of the non-Communist leaders was Foreign Minister Jan Masaryk (1886–1948), son of the late president.

In 1947, Masaryk met personally with Joseph Stalin (1879–1953), dictator of the Soviet Union, who urged him not to accept American aid through the Marshall Plan but to rely on Russia's help. "I went to Moscow as the foreign minister of a sovereign state and I came back a stooge of Stalin," Masaryk later said. When the 11 non-Communist government ministers resigned en masse to protest Soviet influence in their affairs, the Communists simply filled their positions with party members. Fearing the worst was to come, many Czechs began to flee the country. Jan Masaryk, it was rumored, would soon be joining them.

On March 10, 1948, at 6:25 A.M., Masaryk's pajama-clad body was found in the courtyard of his apartment building. It was alleged that he had committed suicide by leaping to his death from his bathroom window, but many Czechs believed that he had been pushed from the window by hired thugs of the Communists to prevent his leaving the country and denouncing them. How Masaryk really died may never be known; in 1969, the Czech Communist government retracted the suicide story and tried to convince the world that the former foreign minister fell to his death accidentally from a window sill while "sitting in a yoga position to combat insomnia."

With most of the leaders of the opposition gone, the Czech Communists went to work recruiting people into their party. By the end of 1948, party membership reached 2.5 million, 18 percent of the population. No other country in Eastern Europe outside of the Soviet Union had such a high party membership. The Communists rewrote the Czech constitution to suit their own ends; rather than sign it, President Benes resigned. A broken man, he died three months later.

Farms were collectivized and industry taken over by the Communist state. Private property no longer existed. The "People's Democracy" of Czechoslovakia was a democracy in name only. Personal freedom ended; the country became a police state.

Meanwhile, in nearby Yugoslavia in 1948, Communist leader Marshal Tito (1892–1980), who was born Josip Broz, did the unthinkable: he severed all relations with Stalin.

The Soviet dictator fumed and grumbled, but Tito was too popular with the people of Yugoslavia to be uprooted and replaced by a Soviet puppet. Fearing that other Communist satellite countries might attempt to follow Tito's lead, Stalin decided that the time was right for a crackdown. Ironically, Czechoslovakia, where Stalin should have felt the most secure, received the brunt of his terror. Rudolph Slánský (1901–52), a loyal Stalinist who had arrested hundreds of Czechs in his leader's name, was charged in 1951 with conspiracy with the Jews to overthrow the republic and arrested with 12 other government officials. The resulting "show trials" were a carbon copy of the infamous Moscow trials of the 1930s where Stalin purged the Party and the Soviet Union of so-called "enemies."

Forced to make ridiculous public confessions of their so-called "crimes," Slánský and 10 of his codefendants were found guilty in 1952 and condemned to death. Even in death, they received no dignity from Stalin's executioners, as this excerpt from an article that appeared in a liberal Prague periodical in 1968 makes clear:

When the eleven condemned had been executed, Referent D. [person being interviewed] found himself, by chance, at the Ruzyn with the [Soviet] adviser Golkin. Present at the meeting were the driver and the two referents who had been charged with the disposal of the ashes. They announced they had placed them inside a potato sack and that they left for the vicinity of Prague with the intention of spreading the ashes in the fields. Noticing the ice-covered pavement, they laughed as he told that it had never before happened to him to be transporting fourteen persons at the same time in his Tatra [kind of automobile], the three living and the eleven contained in the sack.

In all, 180 politicians were executed in the purge trials and an estimated 130,000 ordinary Czechs were arrested, imprisoned and sent to labor camps or executed between 1948 and 1953.

Tomás Masaryk (1850–1937)

Václav Havel, president of the Czech Republic, is not the first writer-thinker to be the leader of his people. He was preceded by Czechoslovakia's founder and first president, Tomás Masaryk. An author and philosophy professor, Masaryk's thoughts on democracy and freedom helped make his homeland Europe's model democracy during his long presidency.

A professor of philosophy and sociology at Charles University, Tomás Masaryk used his ideas and theories on government to transform Czechoslovakia into a model democracy in the two decades between the world wars. (The Bettmann Archive)

Then in March 1953, Joseph Stalin died of a cerebral hemorrhage. The terror subsided as Stalin's lieutenants struggled for power. Nikita Khrushchev (1894–1971), the man who emerged as the new leader of the Soviet Union, denounced Stalin for some of his crimes against humanity in a "secret speech" delivered in 1956. The process of de-Stalinization—the end of Stalin hero-worship and subsequent liberalization of communism—had less effect in Czechoslovakia than in Hungary, Poland and other Communist countries. Unfortunately, the people who had done Stalin's bidding were still in power in Czechoslovakia.

What little light penetrated Czechoslovakia's Iron Curtain was shut out when Antonín Novotný (1904–1975), general secretary of the Czech Communist Party, became president, replacing Antonín Zápotocký (1884–1957), who died. Novotný was a hardline Stalinist who toed the

Masaryk was born in Moravia and his father was the coachman to the Austrian emperor Francis Joseph. He studied at the universities of Vienna and Leipzig and married an American, Charlotte Garrigue. In 1882, Masaryk became professor of philosophy at the new Czech University of Prague, where he began a distinguished career as a teacher, thinker and author.

A member of the Austro-Hungarian parliament from 1891, Masaryk became an outspoken supporter of the rights of the Czechs and Slovaks. Nine years later, he launched the Czech Peoples Party, which called for the unity of the Czechs and Slovaks and national recognition from the Hapsburgs. When World War I broke out, he fled to Switzerland and then England. The Austro-Hungarian government sentenced Masaryk in absentia to death for high treason. Reaching America, he promoted independence for his country to President Woodrow Wilson.

At the war's end, Masaryk helped found Czechoslovakia out of the ruins of the Austro-Hungarian Empire and became its president. For 17 years, his wise and judicious leadership kept his nation in peace and prosperity, although the Slovaks were increasingly unhappy with his failure to recognize their rights more fully. In failing health, Masaryk resigned from office in 1935 and died two years later, mercifully spared the sight of his beloved country becoming a satellite, first to Nazi Germany and then to the Soviet Union.

Alexander Dubcek (1921–92)

"It's been a hard life, but you cannot suppress an idea," said Alexander Dubcek when, after 20 years in exile, his life's work was finally vindicated.

Dubcek's idea of a socialism that met the needs of his country's people challenged the authority of his Soviet masters for one shining moment, as no Eastern European government had before.

Dubcek was not a likely person to reform the communist system: he'd been born in the small Slovakian town of Uhrover to a father who was a cabinet-maker and a founding member of the Czech Communist Party

The jubilation expressed by Czech leader Alexander Dubcek in this May 1968 photo would be short-lived. A few months later, a Soviet invasion ended his liberal reforms, and he was taken to Moscow in handcuffs. (The Bettmann Archive)

party line and quickly alienated his own people. By concentrating on the heavy industry the Soviets required and ignoring consumer products, Novotný helped created a serious recession in the early 1960s. Political unrest, spurred on by students and intellectuals, forced Novotný to make concessions and even get rid of other hardliners in his government.

But the demonstrations continued. By late 1967, it was clear to Leonid Brezhnev (1906–82), Khrushchev's successor in the Kremlin, that Novotný could not control his people and would have to go. In January 1968, he was replaced as party general secretary by a mild-mannered 46-year-old in 1925. The family lived in the Soviet Union for more than a decade, returning in 1938 just before the Nazi invasion. Young Dubcek joined the Communist Party the following year, although it had been outlawed by the Nazis. He worked in the anti-Nazi underground and fought in the Slovak National Uprising in 1944. During the fighting, he was wounded twice and his brother was killed.

After the war, Dubcek was a loyal and hard-working party member who rose through the ranks to become the secretary of the Central Committee of the Communist Party in Slovakia in 1962. When Party leader Novotný resigned in January 1968, Dubcek was unanimously elected by the Central Committee to replace him, becoming the first Slovak to head Czechoslovakia's Communist Party.

Dubcek was chosen because he had no enemies and would offend no one. Some politicians thought he would be easy to manipulate, but they quickly discovered otherwise. Once in power, Dubcek began to initiate far-ranging reforms in the Communist system to give this nation, in his words, "socialism with a human face."

Under Dubcek's liberal rule, the economy experimented with a free-market system, trade was initiated with the West, censorship ended and the arts and intellectualism were encouraged. "Prague Spring," however, proved to be a short season: On August 21, 1968, the Soviet invasion of Czechoslovakia began and Dubcek was taken to Moscow. He returned home a week later a broken man. The reforms soon ended, and in 1970 Dubcek was expelled from the party. He lived in obscurity in Bratislava, the Slovak capital, for nearly two decades.

When communism finally fell, however, the new leaders of the country remembered his achievement and recalled him to Prague, where he served in the Havel government until his sudden death in 1992 at age 70, resulting from a car accident.

Slovak, Alexander Dubcek (see boxed biography). Little was known about Dubcek, other than he was a devoted, lifelong Communist and had a personal integrity that most of his corrupt colleagues lacked.

Prague Spring and Its Bitter Aftermath

In a few short weeks, it was apparent that Dubcek would be a very different kind of Communist leader than the men who had preceded him.

In a speech before a group of Czech farmers, he urged them to take the initiate to improve their lives and then opened the floor to hear their complaints and suggestions. When they spoke against party policy, Dubcek listened. This open forum was repeated throughout the country in the weeks and months ahead. Dubcek soon ended censorship: writers, editors and publishers were free to print the truth about the past, investigate the problems of the present and lay down new plans for the future. The government approved experiments in a mixed economy that allowed for private as well as state businesses. Czechoslovakia increased its trade and dialogue with the Western nations. All these reforms were part of Dubcek's goal of creating "socialism with a human face." After 20 years of the long, dark winter of Communist suppression, Dubcek had opened the window and let in some sunlight and fresh air to his country. People called it "Prague Spring."

Just as Stalin had feared that Yugoslavia's break with the Soviet Union would inspire other countries to do the same, Brezhnev feared the liberalization of Czechoslovakia would encourage the governments of Poland, Hungary and other Soviet satellites to enact reforms. Dubcek insisted that he had no such motive in mind and that what worked for the Czechs would not work elsewhere, but Brezhnev remained skeptical.

In truth, what Dubcek was establishing in Czechoslovakia was the kind of socialism that the Soviets had given lip service to for years—a form of government where the needs of people came first. But the hypocrisy of the Communist system, in which a privileged few held absolute power over the masses, could not stand being shown for the sham it was. In that sense, Brezhnev had good reason to fear Prague Spring.

Then in May 1968, Czech writer Ludvík Vaculík (1926–) published a manifesto that was like a gauntlet flung down before the Soviets. In *The 2,000 Words,* which thousands of Czechs and Slovaks signed, Vaculik condemned the Communist Party for a betrayal of trust.

"The inconstant line of the leadership," wrote Vaculik, "changed the party from a political party and an ideological alliance into a power organization that became very attractive to egotists avid for rule, calculating cowards and unprincipled people."

Brezhnev was aghast. He ordered Dubcek to publicly condemn the manifesto. When he didn't, the Czech president was told to come to Moscow; Dubcek politely declined the invitation. The two men did meet a few weeks later, but neither would budge on his stand. Dubcek returned home, convinced that Brezhnev would not attempt to interfere with his reforms.

But at 10:30 P.M. on Tuesday, August 20, 1968, Soviet warplanes landed at Prague's Ruzyne Airport. Armed Soviet soldiers effectively took over the airport. Within hours, more than 200,000 troops from five Warsaw Pact countries descended on Czechoslovakia. By dawn, Soviet tanks were rolling into the capital. Prague Spring was over and a chilling Soviet winter was returning to the land.

Dubcek and several high officials in his government were arrested and flown to Moscow in handcuffs. They were questioned and put in prison. Brezhnev hoped the Czech people would greet the soldiers as liberators; instead, they saw them for what they were—invaders. A Czech journalist depicted the grim scene in Prague's Wenceslas Square the afternoon of the first full day of the Soviet takeover:

> Over Venohradska Street the smoke from burning houses still rises into the sky. We pass a smoke-smudged youth carrying a sad souvenir—the shell of an 85-mm gun. The fountain below the museum splashes quietly, just as it did yesterday, as if nothing had happened, but when you raise your eyes to the facade of the museum, you freeze in your steps. Against the dark background shine hundreds of white spots, as if evil birds had pecked at the facade. . . . "Soldiers, go home! Quickly!" implores an inscription in Russian fastened to the pedestal of St. Wenseslaus's statue. And below, around the statue, silently sit the young and the old. Saint Wenseslaus is decorated with Czechoslovak flags. . . . People sit dejectedly on the pedestal. On the street corner, small groups of people listen to transistor radios.

Nearly 200 Czechs and Slovaks were killed during the invasion, and hundreds were wounded in clashes with troops. The Western nations, including the United States, condemned the invasion. So did several Communist countries, including Yugoslavia, China and North Vietnam. But no one tried to stop it. The Czechs were left to deal with their tragedy as best they could. Dubcek returned home after a few days, a sad and broken man. He remained president for the time being—his popularity with the people made it difficult for even Brezhnev to remove him. But the reforms he spearheaded came to an end.

The despair and frustration the Czech people felt was dramatically symbolized by Jan Palach, a 21-year-old student. On a cold day in

Many Czechs and Slovaks reacted with defiance to the Soviet invasion of Czechoslovakia in August 1968. Here, a young girl shouts, "Ivan, go home!" to a pair of Russian soldiers sitting stolidly on a tank in a Prague street. (The Bettmann Archive)

mid-January 1969, Palach drenched himself with gasoline and set himself on fire as an act of protest. Although the authorities moved his body to an unknown location, his memory would not be forgotten. Palach was hailed by the people as a martyr to Soviet tyranny.

In April, Dubcek was replaced as first secretary by his colleague Gustav Husák (1913–91). Husák, a victim of Stalin, had learned his lesson and embraced the party line; he would remain in power for 20 years. Dubcek was demoted to ambassador to Turkey and eventually went home to Bratislava, the Slovak capital. He took a job as a mechanic for the Forestry Department to support his family and remained in obscurity until he retired in 1981.

Years of Protest,
Years of Change

Husák and the hardliners in Prague might control the country, but they could not push the economy forward. In the 1970s, economic stagnation grew worse and inflation soared. Students and intellectuals again led demonstrations and protests. One of the leaders of the protest movement was Czech playwright Václav Havel (see boxed biography, Chapter 4). During the relaxation of censorship in the sixties, Havel had become celebrated for his dark comedies that satirized the Communist bureaucracy. With the end of Prague Spring, Havel became a nonperson, his works forbidden to be performed or published. In January 1977, he helped found the human rights movement called Charter 77. The organization gave a focus to Czech resistance and was a real threat to the Communists. One Charter 77 leader, Jan Patocka, died mysteriously after being detained by the police. Havel was arrested in October 1979, charged with "subversion" and sentenced to four and one-half years at hard labor. He was released 10 months early due to ill health.

In 1985, a new leader came to power in the Soviet Union. Like Dubcek in Czechoslovakia, Mikhail Gorbachev (1931–) brought reform and change to the rigid Communist system. Gorbachev's emphasis on economic reform, a reduction in the military and relaxation of censorship left hardliners like Husák and the Communist leaders in other Eastern Bloc countries suddenly out in the cold. In December 1987, Husák resigned as party leader. However, the stubborn Communists refused to cave in and replaced him with the even more conservative Milos Jakes.

On August 20, 1988—the 20th anniversary of the Soviet invasion —10,000 demonstrators marched in Prague. Police attacked the demonstrators and made arrests. But the unrest was far greater in neighboring Communist countries. The Solidarity trade-union movement in Poland had forced the Communists to the negotiation table. Free elections were in the offing in Poland. Communists, who could no longer count on support of the Soviet Union, were being thrown out of Hungary and Bulgaria. By November of 1989, new democratic governments were firmly in place in Poland, Hungary and East Germany, where the Berlin Wall that had separated Communist East Germany from democratic West Germany for nearly three decades was being torn down. The time for change had come for Czechoslovakia as well. The question was: What form would that change take?

NOTES

pp. 21–22   "The air rages . . . " *The New York Times,* February 20, 1995.

p. 22   "I went to Moscow . . . " Dan Riley, *The People's Almanac #3* (New York: Bantam, 1981), p. 6.

p. 23   "sitting in a yoga position . . . " Dan Riley, *The People's Almanac #3,* p. 9.

p. 24   "When the eleven condemned . . . " Tad Szulc, *Czechoslovakia Since World War II* (New York: Viking, 1971), p. 105.

p. 26   "It's been a hard life, . . . " The *Connecticut Post,* November 8, 1992.

p. 29   "The inconstant line . . . " Ina Navazelskis, *Alexander Dubcek,* (New York: Chelsea House, 1990), p. 87.

p. 29   "Over Venohradska Street . . . " Rude Pravo, quoted in *The Czech Black Book* (New York: Praeger, 1969), pp. 49–50.

4

The Velvet Revolution and the Velvet Divorce (1989–present)

As the authoritarian world they had known for 40 years crumbled around them, the Communist leaders of Czechoslovakia shut their eyes and carried on. Pressured by his people clamoring for freedom and the Soviets, who urged immediate reform, President Jakes loosened restrictions on travel and allowed more freedom of worship and less censorship. On the political front, however, nothing changed.

"The leadership here is dead, only waiting to be carried away," dissident Jiří Dienstbier (1937–) told the *New York Times* in November 1989. "The party's only alternative to the status quo is to open up the system, but they know that once they open it up, they are doomed."

The end, delayed for so long, came with shuddering speed. On November 17, Prague saw the largest political demonstration since Prague Spring of 1968. The demonstrators, at first mostly students and intellectuals, were brutally attacked by the police. This gained them the sympathy and support of the workers. Soon, the crowds in the capital city swelled to more than 200,000. As the demonstrations continued, opposition groups, including Charter 77, met to form one large organization—Civic Forum—"as a spokesman on behalf of that part of the Czechoslovak public which is increasingly critical of the existing Czechoslovak leadership." Desperately losing ground, Jakes and his cohorts agreed to hold talks with Civic Forum and its leader, Václav Havel.

On the sixth day of the demonstrations, a voice from the past lent his weight and authority to the cries for the resignation of the Communist leadership. Alexander Dubcek, now 68 years old, gave his first public speech in 21 years to an audience of 2,000 Slovaks in Bratislava and called for the formation of a new, freely elected government. In a message read later to the people of Prague, he expressed his solidarity with them and his desire to stand with them in Wenceslas Square.

Three days later, on November 24, the Communist leadership resigned, but new Communists replaced them, led by Karel Urbanek, party leader of Bohemia. "The new leadership is a trick that was meant to confuse," said Havel. "The power remains in or is passing into the hands of the neo-Stalinists."

The following day, a Saturday, the demonstrators in Prague numbered 800,000. A two-hour general strike was set for Monday noon by the protest leaders. When the time came, millions of Czech and Slovak workers left their jobs and walked into the streets. For two hours, the entire country shut down. Only hospitals, nursing homes and a few businesses remained open. The people stood and cried in the streets for joy. After decades of frustration, they knew their time had finally come.

"Before this, I was afraid of what would come next," confessed a 21-year-old student. "Our professor told us recently that our country was turning into a memorial display of Communism. But now we have taken our own way."

Demonstrators in Wenceslas Square, the center of the protest movement against the Communists, light candles in November 1989 to symbolize their struggle. Although one of the last Eastern European countries to see the collapse of communism, it experienced one of the most peaceful transitions from authoritarianism to democracy. (The Bettmann Archive)

The final blow came, ironically, from the Soviets. Gorbachev declared the 1968 reform movement of Dubcek had been "a process of democratization, renewal and humanization of society." The Russians not only officially condemned the invasion but also seriously considered the withdrawal of remaining Soviet troops from Czechoslovakia. On December 7, Ladislav Adamec, one of the most moderate of the Communist leaders, resigned as prime minister. His replacement, the Slovak Marián Calfa, was ready to negotiate for a transition of power. Three days later, on International Human Rights Day, a coalition government took power, with the Communists in the minority. Dubcek was named chairman of the national Federal Assembly and on December 29, 1989, this body unanimously elected Václav Havel the country's first non-Communist president in 40 years. Havel said he had no intentions of becoming a politician and promised to step down when a new president could be elected the following year in the country's first free elections since 1946.

The Czech "revolution" was seen as something of a miracle abroad.

Václav Havel (1936–)

The first president of the Czech Republic was born into one of Prague's wealthiest families. His father was a property owner and restauranteur; his uncle owned the largest motion-picture studio in Czechoslovakia. All that changed in 1948 when the Communists took over the country. The new government nationalized business and industry, and overnight the Havels lost everything. The future playwright was denied a university education and was forced to earn a living as a worker in a chemical laboratory.

Determined to get an education, Havel enrolled in night school to get his high school diploma and drove a taxi by day to pay his tuition. Turned down time and again by the university, he got a job as a stagehand at an avant-garde theater in Prague. He progressed from stagehand to electrician, secretary, literary manager and finally playwright. His plays, with their double-talk and absurd humor, mercilessly satirized the Communist system. In 1968, during the Prague Spring, Havel was allowed to visit the

Relaxed, informal and thoughtful, playwright and dissident Václav Havel makes an unlikely presidential candidate in 1989—anywhere else perhaps but in Czechoslovakia. (The Bettmann Archive)

After years of repression, terror and death, the Czechs had ended Communist rule bloodlessly, without a single loss of life. The transfer of power in Prague was peaceful and smooth—so smooth that the world called it "the Velvet Revolution." Few realized the end of communism would quickly lead to the end of Czechoslovakia itself.

first American production of one of his plays in New York City. It was named the best Off-Broadway foreign play of the season.

But with the Soviet invasion in August, Havel once again experienced a complete turnabout. Overnight, Czechoslovakia's most prominent playwright was a nonperson: His plays were banned from the stage and his books forbidden to be published or sold. Havel fought back by becoming a full-time dissident. In the 1970s, he was arrested repeatedly, jailed twice and forced to make a meager living by stacking barrels in a brewery for $50 a week. Continuing his role as a spokesperson for the human rights movement, he was arrested again in October 1979, charged with "subversion" and sentenced to four and one-half years at hard labor. During his imprisonment, Havel almost died from pneumonia, complicated by a lung abscess. The government offered him freedom if he would only request a pardon. Havel refused. Nonetheless, his sentence was suspended due to ill health in early 1983, 10 months short of its completion.

Five years later, the Communist government collapsed and Václav Havel, his country's leading dissident, was the unanimous choice to head the new government. He accepted the honor, determined to make the lives of his people better. "Dear friends, I promise you I will not betray your confidence," he told them.

But the leaders of the two factions in Czechoslovakia appeared to disappoint him. As Czech Prime Minister Václav Klaus and Slovak Prime Minister Vladimír Meciar worked out a plan to divide their country into two separate nations, Havel resigned from the presidency in disgust. With the establishment of the Czech Republic in January 1993, he agreed to run again for president and was elected leader of the new nation.

As Havel told *Time* magazine in an interview in 1992, he is hopeful for the future: " . . . there is a colorful spectrum of possibilities, from the worst to the best. . . . Hope forces me to believe that those better alternatives will prevail, and above all it forces me to do something to make them happen."

Reign of the Philosopher King

Václav Havel cut a strange figure as president of his country. A man of the people, he shunned the trappings of his office in Hradcany Castle, the traditional home of Czech rulers. He appointed intellectuals, fellow writers and artists to his Council of Advisers and sometimes rode around the halls of the castle on a child's scooter. But for all this, Havel took his job seriously. He set about not only reforming the government and establishing democratic freedom and personal rights, but also transforming the planned economy of the Communists to a free-market system where people could run their own businesses and farms.

In February 1990, Havel visited the United States for the first time as president. In an address before the joint houses of the U.S. Congress, he spoke eloquently about his people and his mission:

> . . . The salvation of our world can be found only in the human heart, in the power of humans to reflect, in human meekness and responsibility.
>
> Without a global revolution in the sphere of human consciousness, nothing will change for the better in the sphere of our being as humans, and the catastrophe towards which this world is headed—be it ecological, social, demographic, or a general breakdown of civilization—will be unavoidable. If we are no longer threatened by world war or by the danger of absurd mountains of nuclear weapons blowing up the world, this does not mean that we have finally won. This is actually far from being a final victory. . . .
>
> I shall close by repeating what I said at the beginning: history has accelerated. I believe that once again it will be the human mind that perceives this acceleration, comprehends its shape, and transforms its own words into deeds.

Both at home and abroad, Havel was seen as a national hero, and he decided to run for a full-term as president in elections held in the spring of 1990. He won by a large majority. The Civic Forum, in coalition with another opposition group, Public Against Violence, took 56 percent of the seats in the Federal Assembly, winning out over 20 other parties. The Communist Party, interestingly enough, was the second biggest winner, taking 47 of the 300 seats in the assembly. The country was in a celebratory mood, but under the goodwill and joy, old ethnic divisions and rivalries were beginning to fray the fabric of the Velvet Revolution.

Slovakia Wants to Be Free

In April 1990, Slovak sociologist Fedor Gál was asked in an interview what he thought of the chances of "separatist tendencies" in his region. "It's absurd to think that a small, angry nation like Slovakia has any prospects whatever . . ." he replied. "I'd very much like to be able to label these separatists 'fringe extremists.'"

But by 1992, the extremists seemed to be gaining ground. Vladimír Meciar (1942–), a former Slovak Communist and self-avowed populist, had emerged as the main spokesman for the separatists and head of a new political party, the Movement for a Democratic Slovakia. Meciar argued convincingly that the Slovaks were suffering economically far more than the Czechs in the transition from the planned Communist economy to a free-market one. Long bolstered up by the Soviets, the Slovak economy plummeted with their withdrawal from Czechoslovakian affairs, and unemployment in the region soared to 12 percent. Less industrialized than the Czech lands, Slovakia could not manage for itself in the shifting marketplace. Largely rural, its agricultural economy was outmoded and ill equipped to deal with the free market.

Meciar's campaign touched a sensitive nerve with all Slovaks. The resentment they felt towards their better-educated and more-affluent Czech cousins had deep roots. Ever since the formation of Czechoslovakia in 1918, the Czechs had politically dominated the Slovaks, denying them full representation in the government and most often telling them what to do. This bossy, unattractive side of the Czech character was matched by the stubborn, proud side of the Slovaks. After more than 70 years of Czech and Communist domination, the Slovaks were ready for a change. Now, with the bonds of communism broken, Meciar was calling for independence for Slovakia. He threatened to block Havel's reelection as president by running against him in the upcoming national elections of June 1992. If he won control of the Slovak Parliament, Meciar threatened to call for a referendum on the issue of separation. Havel considered

Meciar and his party as opportunists out to gain power for themselves. He claimed that such a split between Czechs and Slovaks would lead to political chaos and urged both peoples not to cast their vote "for people for whom power is more important than the fate of the nation. . . ."

In an election in which 90 percent of Czechoslovaks turned out to vote, Meciar's party took one-third of the Slovak vote, while close to half of all Czech votes were cast for the right-wing coalition centered around Finance Minister Václav Klaus (1941–), head of the new Civic Democratic Party. The former Communists trailed in third place with 13 percent of the vote. The political lines had been drawn. Klaus, who became prime minister shortly after, saw the future of the country moving swiftly away from socialism to a free-market economy. Meciar, elected prime minister of Slovakia, saw this rush to democracy as devastating to his country's economy and refused to accept Klaus's policies.

The determined faces of Czech Prime Minister Václav Klaus and his Slovak counterpart Vladimír Meciar foreshadow the coming split of Czechoslovakia into two independent republics. Here, they sit together during the funeral of Czech religious leader Cardinal Frantisek Tomasek in August 1992.
(The Bettmann Archive)

The Velvet Divorce

On July 17, 1992, the Slovak National Council adopted a declaration of sovereignty in a vote of 113 to 24. Three days later, President Havel resigned, refusing to preside over the dissolution of his country.

Czech Prime Minister Klaus met with Meciar, and the two men negotiated what a short time before most of their compatriots thought unthinkable—the dissolution of their state. On November 25, the Federal Assembly of Czechoslovakia voted the split to go into effect at midnight on December 31. While many Czechs and Slovaks did not feel as repulsed as Havel did over the division, only a few enthusiastically supported it. In a *New York Times* poll taken in the fall of 1992, only 37 percent of Slovaks and 36 percent of Czechs said they would vote for the split in a referendum; yet more than 80 percent saw such a split as inevitable and were resigned to it.

Like the Velvet Revolution, the Velvet Divorce was peaceful and completed with little disruption. With only 50,000 Czechs living in Slovakia and 300,000 Slovaks in the Czech Republic, there was no great uprooting of populations. All territorial claims were dismissed; land was the property of the republic it was located in. Special commissions were set up to divide other property on the basis of population size and a ratio of 2 (Czech Republic) to 1 (Slovak Republic). Military personnel were allowed to serve the republic to which they felt most loyal.

With the split, the government of Prime Minister Klaus moved its economic reform forward with more speed. Václav Havel reentered the political arena and ran for the presidency of the Czech Republic. He easily beat his two opponents and was sworn into office on February 2, 1993. Politically more liberal than Klaus, Havel is often at odds with his prime minister.

As Klaus attended to the economy and internal affairs, Havel reached out to strengthen bonds with new friends and former enemies abroad. In August 1993, Russian president Boris Yeltsin (1931–) visited Prague and met with Havel to sign a treaty with the new republic on the 25th anniversary of the Soviet invasion. The new treaty, Havel said, provided the "psychological and political climate" for closer relations between the two countries. Yeltsin, for his part, condemned the 1968 invasion and laid flowers on a memorial to Czech women shot by Soviet soldiers while waiting for a tram in Prague during the invasion.

In January 1994, American President Bill Clinton (1946–) met with Havel and other leaders of Eastern Europe. While Havel's relationship with the United States remained a positive one, he expressed frustration over the U.S.'s refusal to allow his country into the North Atlantic Treaty Organization (NATO)*, which many Czechs believe would strengthen ties with the West and stave off any future threat from Russia.

During 1994, the privatization of state-owned companies continued at an accelerated rate. Klaus had hit upon a unique way to entice the public to become a part of this process: The government issued booklets of vouchers that adults could buy for $35 and use either to bid for shares in independent state companies or to invest in new mutual funds.

While the program largely succeeded, the prime minister's critics pointed out that a large number of the newly privatized companies carried large debts held by state banks, a glaring conflict of interest that could upset the economy and lead to bankruptcy. At the end of 1994, the head of the voucher program was arrested for carrying $286,000 in a suitcase and was charged with bribery. Klaus later reassigned the man to a job in the tax office.

Called by some "the toughest leader of Post-Communism's biggest success story," Klaus continues to stir up controversy as he moves his country down the road to capitalism. He has proposed that students pay fees for a university education, something never considered under the Communists. "Every investment costs something," he explains. "If you want to invest, you have to pay something first. Then you get your money back."

To illustrate his point further, Klaus has questioned the social security program in the Czech Republic and introduced legislation to raise the retirement age for men from 62 to 65 and for women from 55 to 62.

So far, Klaus's rather autocratic way of governing has not caused him widespread disfavor with the public, but whatever the future holds politically, the Czech Republic promises to have one of the brightest futures in Eastern Europe when the transition from communism to democracy is at last complete.

---

* An organization formed in 1949 composed mostly of Western European countries and the United States for mutual defense if any one nation is attacked.

NOTES

p. 34   "The leadership here is dead, . . . " Bernard Gwertzman and Michael T. Kaufman, *The Collapse of Communism* (New York: Times Books, 1990), p. 226.

p. 34   "as a spokesman . . . " Gale Stokes, *The Walls Came Tumbling Down: The Collapse of Communism in Eastern Europe* (New York: Oxford University Press, 1993), p. 156.

p. 34   "The new leadership . . . " Gwertzman and Kaufman, *The Collapse of Communism,* p. 237.

p. 34   "Before this, I was afraid . . . " Gwertzman and Kaufman, *The Collapse of Communism,* pp. 265–66.

p. 37   "Dear friends, . . . " Gwertzman and Kaufman, *The Collapse of Communism,* p. 344.

p. 37   ". . . there is a colorful spectrum . . . " *Time,* August 3, 1992, p. 48.

p. 38   "The salvation of our world . . . " Václav Havel, "Address to a Joint Session of the United States Congress," *After The Velvet Revolution* (London: Freedom House, 1991), pp. 78, 80.

p. 39   "separatist tendencies . . . . It's absurd . . . " Fedor Gal, "Slovakia's Problems and Prospects," *After The Velvet Revolution* (London: Freedom House, 1991), pp. 231–32.

p. 40   "for people for whom . . . " *The New York Times,* June 6, 1992.

p. 41   "psychological and political climate," *The New York Times,* August 27, 1993.

p. 42   "the toughest leader . . ." Jane Perlez, "The First in the Velvet Glove," *The New York Times Magazine,* July 16, 1995, p. 17.

p. 42   "Every investment costs something . . . " Jane Parlez, *The New York Times Magazine,* p. 17

5

Government

It is not surprising that democracy has taken firmer root in the soil of the Czech Republic than in that of any of its neighbors in Eastern Europe. No other country in the region has had as much experience with this form of government. The nearly two-decade administration of Tomás Masaryk was the shining example of democracy in Central Europe between the world wars. The liberal socialist experiment of the Dubcek government in 1968 challenged 20 years of Communist rule. Although it was quickly crushed, it was not forgotten. The intellectual-led human rights movement of the 1980s was driven by democratic ideals and a burning desire for a free and open society.

The government that was founded by the Czechs and Slovaks in the wake of communism's downfall was one anchored in this rich democratic past. It is no accident that the Czech Republic, alone among the former Eastern Bloc countries, has remained politically stable and staunchly democratic since 1989. In Poland, Hungary, Bulgaria and Romania, ex-Communists have returned to power, elected by people tired of reform and fearful of a still uncertain future. The former Yugoslavia and several republics of the former Soviet Union have been rocked by civil war, ethnic bloodshed and political chaos. Yet, life in the Czech Republic goes forward in peace and relative prosperity. This situation led Czech foreign minister Josef Zieleniec to remark in 1994 that Czech news appeared nearly nowhere outside the country but in the business sections of foreign newspapers.

This comment hardly seems an exaggeration. In mid-1995, unemployment in the Czech Republic was the lowest in Europe at 3.3 percent. The country had a healthy budget surplus of $400 million, and inflation was holding at 10 percent, modest by Eastern European standards. The "Velvet Recovery," as its chief architect Prime Minister Václav Klaus calls it, is a pragmatic mix of shock-therapy economics and soft-pedalled socialism. In many ways, Klaus is an arch-capitalist, but he has not burned all his bridges with the Communist past. Subsidies for electricity and heating continue, as do rent controls. Workers are kept employed in state-owned factories, although they have little work to do. By keeping the safety nets of socialism in place, Klaus has largely avoided the painful symptoms—soaring inflation, high unemployment and a lower standard of living—that have gone with the transition from a planned economy to a free-market one elsewhere in Eastern Europe and brought dissatisfaction with reform.

"For achieving something you must first have a vision and politicians who are able to sell the vision to their citizens . . ." he has said. "The Czech Republic is the only [post-Communist country] with well-defined political parties."

Klaus came to power in 1993 supported by the largest and probably best-defined political party in the Czech Republic today—the Civic Democratic Party–Christian Democratic Party coalition. This conservative-centrist four-party coalition won a majority of nearly 30 percent of the vote in the earlier federal parliamentary election in June 1992. The only other party with any real clout is the more moderate Social Democratic Party, led by Milos Zeman, one of Klaus's severest critics. The Social Democrats have been gaining steadily in public opinion polls in 1995 and will undoubtedly make a bid for power in the 1996 parliamentary elections.

The Two Václavs—
A Study in Contrast

The Klaus government sees itself as an integral part of Western Europe. This pride in Western traditions and a deep desire to join the democracies of the West is a feeling Klaus shares with Václav Havel, the Czech Republic's first president, but here, the similarities between these two political leaders end. Havel is an idealist, an intellectual and an artist. For him, moral and ethical issues are as important as a robust economy and a stable government. While pleased with the material success that has been the fruit of the democratization of his country, he is deeply concerned with the problems that prosperity is bringing to his country. These problems, some of which will be examined in more detail in the

Bridging the world of politics and literature, President Havel (center) poses in New York on a 1990 visit with, from the left, novelist Kurt Vonnegut, Jr., playwright Arthur Miller, New York City Mayor David Dinkins, producer Joseph Papp and playwright Edward Albee. (The Bettmann Archive)

last chapter of this book, include corruption and greed that extends from Prague cab drivers who overcharge tourists to politicians who take bribes. Other problems are intolerance and racism toward minorities and a careless attitude toward the environment.

" . . . We have no reason to rejoice about the spiritual and moral state of our society . . ." Havel has said. "It is not enough to rely on the automatic effect of a stabilized political and economic system."

Klaus, on the other hand, has no fear of a future where the principle of laissez-faire rules. His philosophy is "Create the conditions for a market economy to function normally, and the rest, independent formation of a civil society, will take care of itself."

A graduate of the Prague School of Economics with a specialty in foreign commerce, Klaus is a conservative who favors dark business suits (Havel wears jeans to work). He was openly critical of the "socialist market" economics in the 1960s and was fired from his job at the Academy of Sciences' Economic Institute because of his Western political views. Like Havel, he had to work his way back up the career ladder through menial jobs eventually to become a member of the Institute for Economic Forecasting in the Academy of Sciences in 1988.

His critical views of the Communists' economic program found much support. He became finance minister in the new democratic government in December 1989 and was chairman of the Civic Forum in October 1990.

A proud nationalist, some observers believe Klaus allowed Slovak leader Vladimír Meciar to push for a break with the Czechs because he wanted to be freed of the burden of carrying the more agricultural and backward Slovak economy. Many Czechs are cynical about Klaus, but the public still supports him because his policies have largely worked.

Among the prime minister's strongest critics is former Foreign Minister Jiří Dienstbier, who Klaus pushed out of office because he was too outspoken and not a team player. A former political prisoner and leading dissident like Havel, Dienstbier is one of the most popular politicians in the Czech Republic today and one of the few men who could conceivably replace Klaus as prime minister. Dienstbier accuses Klaus of running "an authoritarian state," pointing to the fact that he refused to agree to the formation of an upper house of Parliament, even though the 1992 Constitution called for it.

Dienstbier also criticizes the Klaus government for its questionable ethics: " . . . there's more corruption because there's more money," he says. "The communists were totally corrupt, but now we've got a private-enterprise mafia and, like all private enterprise, it's better."

These accusations are not just the empty charges of a bitter political rival. Charges of bribery, corruption and political dirty tricks have been made against several government officials. Deputy Prime Minister Jan Kalvoda, a member of the Civic Democratic Alliance party, accused the state intelligence agency of spying on his party's activities in January of 1995 in order to find political dirt to use against them in the upcoming parliamentary elections.

The situation grew so bad that on March 22, President Havel called a meeting of the four-party coalition leaders to avert further political damage and a possible break-up of the coalition. "Disputes, rivalry and tension between coalition parties produce no benefits and would result in making the country's political leadership untrustworthy and arousing people's mistrust of politicians," he said.

Yet Havel himself is not untainted by public mistrust. While still admired for his moral leadership, he has been heavily criticized by many for his failure to prevent the division of Czechoslovakia. Rather than walk away from the situation, they feel Havel should have taken a stronger stand against the impending split. Another reason that Havel's heroic image has been slightly tarnished of late is his new economic status. A member of one of Czechoslovakia's richest families, Havel lost everything when the Communists came to power. Now, with a government restitution program in effect, he has regained much of the prime real estate his family formerly owned and is worth at least $30 million. The president who derided the ornateness of Hradcany Castle now owns a $1-million villa behind it.

Foreign Policy

If any issue joins the often battling Václavs together, it may be foreign policy. "We are in the heart of Europe," Klaus declared at a World Economic Forum. "We belong to Europe; what you would call the Western world and I call the standard world. No third way."

To become closer to the West, both Klaus and Havel have joined other Eastern European leaders in asking for membership in NATO (see Chapter 4). Although the Clinton administration looks favorably on accepting these

The Communists

While the Velvet Revolution was a bloodless one, in its aftermath many Czechs and Slovaks believed that the Communists and their collaborators should be punished for their crimes against the people of Czechoslovakia. In 1991, the Czechoslovak Parliament passed a controversial law that barred many Communists and those who helped them maintain order from holding high positions in industry and business for five years. The careers and livelihoods of hundreds of thousands of Czechs and Slovaks were affected.

The problem with the law is the difficulty of determining who is guilty of collaboration. Some accusations appear to be based on personal motives as much as on documented fact. Of the 20 Parliament members identified by the government as Communist informers, 11 have fought the charges against them in court. One of the most vocal victims is Josef Bartoncik, leader of the independent People's Party, which the Communists allowed to exist during their reign. Bartoncik denied being an informer for the secret police, and in Parliamentary elections in 1992 kept his seat. His party, however, lost half of its support, getting only 10 percent of the vote.

Among those who would like to see the law against Communists repealed is President Václav Havel. He believes that it is destructive to the future to dwell on the past. "A good number of people are fed up with the past," writes Czech intellectual Jan Urban. "We have to look forward. . . . After 40 to 50 years of totalitarianism, there's so much dirt behind us. After looking professionally at our past, we just have to say: Enough."

countries, the financial and human cost in sending troops to secure and possibly to defend Eastern Europe in the event of war make such acceptance doubtful in the immediate future. Besides this, all 16 members of the organization must give their unanimous approval before the Czech Republic, Poland, Hungary and other countries can be accepted.

However, a powerful lobby of 23-million Americans of Eastern European descent will probably exert considerable pressure on the next U.S. president, whoever he may be. As Clinton said in Prague on a visit in early 1994, acceptance by NATO was not "a question of whether . . . but when and how."

While the Czech Republic has remained friendly with Russia and the former republics of the Soviet Union, it has also made no bones about its

Czech Republic: Physical Features

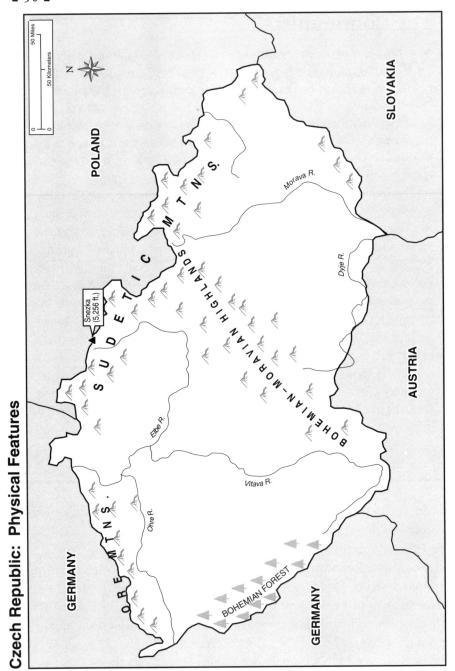

POLAND

SLOVAKIA

AUSTRIA

GERMANY

GERMANY

S U D E T I C   M T N S.

O R E   M T N S.

BOHEMIAN-MORAVIAN HIGHLANDS

BOHEMIAN FOREST

Snezka
(5,256 ft.)

Morava R.

Dyje R.

Elbe R.

Ohre R.

Vitava R.

N

50 Miles

50 Kilometers

intolerance for communism, which still exists in other parts of the world. When Prime Minister Lien Chan of Taiwan, the last outpost of the Nationalist, anticommunist Chinese, made an unprecedented trip to the Czech Republic, Austria and Hungary in June 1995, Václav Klaus was the only head of state to meet with him. This so incensed the Communist government of mainland China that it cut short the visit of a Chinese education delegation to the Czech Republic and threatened further diplomatic action.

The Three Branches
of the Federal Government

"The political structure is more European than American, with more than two political parties, which results in a coalition government and standard pressure between the cabinet and parliament," explained Pime Minister Klaus, describing his government in an acceptance speech for the International Democracy Medal for 1995. According to this European model, the Czech president, while head of state, does not run the government. He does play an important role in representing his country at home and abroad. He is also the commander in chief of the armed forces. The president is elected for a five-year term by both houses of parliament.

It is the prime minister who runs the government. He is named by the president but at the suggestion of the speaker of the legislature. He may remain in power until his party loses the nation's confidence or is voted out of office. Klaus, who remains highly respected, if not loved, by the people, seems to face little chance of that happening soon.

The legislative branch, called Parliament, is made up of two separate chambers, not unlike our own Congress. Under the new constitution of January 1, 1993, the House of Representatives consists of 400 members, elected for four-year terms, proportionally representing their districts. The Senate is made up of 81 members, who are elected for six-year terms, one per district.

The judiciary branch of government, which was established a year and a half before the other two branches, consists of four kinds of courts—civil, criminal, commercial and administrative.

Criminal cases are usually handled by district courts ruled by a judge and two associate judges. Associate judges are elected for four-year terms and are drawn from citizens above the age of 25. Cases can be appealed to higher courts up to the country's Supreme Court. There is no death penalty in the Czech Republic.

Administrative courts handle cases appealed by citizens who question the legality of decisions of state institutions. Commercial courts examine disputes in business matters. These cases can often be the most intriguing of all because the laws in the commercial arena are as yet poorly defined. A good example is in the area of trademarks: Toyota, the Japanese car manufacturer, is fighting Czech entrepreneur Marek Nemec, who since 1990 has been using the Toyota name to sell Chinese-made sewing machines. Under Czech law, Nemec has been free to use the name because he is the first person in the country to register it. Since then, Nemec has bought up at least 30 other trademarks, including Chevrolet, Ramada and Kawasaki, and has applied for 50 more. Nemec's brother Igor, who happens to be the prime minister's chief of staff, claims no involvement in his brother's wheeler-dealing. "The question is whether we need a new law or can we upgrade the old law," says Igor Nemec. "It's very clear a change is necessary."

Local Government

The Czech Republic is divided into eight administrative regions, or *kraj*. One region is the capital, Prague. Other regional seats include the cities of Pilsen, Brno and Ostrava.

District bureaus have replaced the national committees that once ran regional and local government under the communist system. These bureaus have the power to raise local taxes. They oversee the building and maintaining of roadways, public health, utilities and the school system. Nevertheless, their power is strictly limited by the national government of the Civic Democrats.

"They [the Czechs] have democracy at a macro-level, but there's a lack of decentralization of political power," points out Stephen Heinz of the Institute for East-West Studies in Prague. "But in this country, which was a democratic country with a long history of democracy, it's not such an alarming situation as it might be elsewhere in the region."

The stability of their government will allow Czech leaders to make errors and mistakes in governing, but if they don't work together to correct the excesses of a smug, sometimes all-too-complacent government, the results could be damaging, not just for those who govern, but for all Czechs.

NOTES

p. 45   "For achieving something . . . " *Forbes,* June 20, 1994, p. 76.

p. 47   ". . . We have no reason . . . " *The Christian Science Monitor,* December 7, 1994.

p. 47   "Create the conditions . . . " *The Christian Science Monitor,* December 7, 1994.

p. 47   "an authoritarian state," Jane Perlez, "The Fist in the Velvet Glove," *The New York Times Magazine,* July 16, 1995, p. 19.

p. 47   ". . . there's more corruption . . . " *The Chicago Tribune,* October 12, 1994.

p. 48   "Disputes rivalry and tension . . . " Reuters, April 6, 1995.

p. 48   "we are in the heart . . . " *Forbes,* June 20, 1994, p. 76.

p. 49   "A good number of people . . . " Stephen Engelberg, "The Velvet Revolution Gets Rough," *The New York Times Sunday Magazine,* May 31, 1992, p. 54.

p. 49   "a question of whether . . . " *The Washington Post,* July 7, 1995.

p. 51   "The political structure . . . " *The Congressional Record,* May 9, 1995.

p. 52   "The question is whether . . . " *The New York Times,* February 19, 1995.

pp. 52–53   "They [the Czechs] have democracy . . ." *The Christian Science Monitor,* May 24, 1995.

6

Religion

In a country where religion has historically played a leading role since saints Cyril and Methodius first brought Christianity to it about 700 A.D., the Czech Republic is today a surprisingly apathetic nation when it comes to organized religion. While nearly 40 percent of the population is practicing Roman Catholic, an equal percentage profess no religious affiliation or are Catholic in name only. The remaining 20 percent are mostly Protestant, with 15,000 Jews and a small number of followers of the Czech Orthodox Church. One possible reason for the decline in faith is the 40-year reign of communism.

Religion Under the Communists

When the Communists took over Czechoslovakia in 1948, their policy toward religion was similar to that taken in other Eastern European countries behind the Iron Curtain: While the atheistic Communists were strongly antireligious, they did allow Czechs to worship in church and to give religious instruction to schoolchildren on church premises. Priests and ministers were generally allowed to conduct baptisms, weddings and funerals, and religious materials such as educational instruction and hymnbooks could be published but were subject to the same censorship that existed for all publications.

Believers throughout the country, however, could not become Communist Party members and could not work in government service. Antireligious propaganda was a part of the curriculum in all Communist-controlled schools.

By the mid- to late 1950s, after Stalin's death, restrictions on religious worship were loosened, and a surprising dialogue began in Eastern Europe between Marxist thinkers and Christian theologians, trying to find common ground on which to express themselves. Czechoslovakia was in the forefront of this dialogue, and in 1967 the only Christian-Marxist congress ever held in Eastern Europe took place at Mariánské-Lázne, Czechoslovakia.

The following year, during Prague Spring, Alexander Dubcek removed nearly all restrictions on religious activities. The Bureau of Religious Affairs, whose main purpose previously had been to thwart religious instruction, now became an agency to further cooperation between the Socialist state and the churches.

While churchgoers tended to be old people who clung to the faith in which they had been raised before the Communists took over, the protest movement of the 1980s, led by Václav Havel and others, prompted more and more young Czechs and Slovaks to search for a faith in something bigger than themselves. Havel described this spiritual renewal in his book-length interview *Disturbing the Peace:*

> . . . The endless, unchanging wasteland of the herd life in a socialist consumer society, its intellectual and spiritual vacuity, its moral sterility, necessarily causes young people to turn their attentions somewhere further and higher; it compels them . . . to look for a more meaningful system of values and standards, to seek, among the diffuse and fragmented world of frenzied consumerism (where goods are hard to come by) for a point that will hold firm. . . .

Yet, the religious revival did not catch fire in Czechoslovakia as it did in Poland, where the Catholic Church provided a moral leadership that kept the people's minds and hearts intact. Part of the reason for this was that the church was more suppressed in Czechoslovakia than in Poland, where it historically was stronger and more resistant to persecution. Another reason was the Roman Catholic Church's association with the Austro-Hungarian Empire, which dominated the Czech and Slovak lands in the 20th century. Viewing the church as part of the powerful state that was suppressing them, millions of Czechs and Slovaks left the Catholic Church between the two world wars. Some joined Protestant denominations, but many more became indifferent to organized religion.

A lapsed Catholic, Havel's mixed feelings about organized religion are shared by a large number of Czechs. Here, he is greeted by American Cardinal John O'Connor and Rabbi Arthur Schneier outside St. Patrick's Cathedral in New York City. (The Bettmann Archive)

Nonetheless, in the mid-1980s, one courageous clergyman stepped forward to defy the Communists and unite the faithful. Cardinal Frantisek Tomasek invited Polish Pope John Paul II to Czechoslovakia to help celebrate the 1100th anniversary of the death of Saint Methodius. Although the government refused permission for the pope's visit, more than 100,000 Czechs and Slovaks flocked to the celebration held at Velehrad. Targeted by the party press for his stand against the government, Cardinal Tomasek wrote with characteristic Czech wit the following response in an open letter: "The church here is not the center of political opposition. All it wishes to do is carry on its pastoral and missionary work. . . . Talking of peace and disarmament would only become relevant and effective when justice and respect for human rights prevail."

Cardinal Tomasek continued to support human rights in his country, and on November 24, 1989, as protest demonstrations in Prague swelled, he conducted a mass celebrating the canonization of Bohemia's patron saint, Agnes Premyslid. The service was broadcast on television and drew tens of thousands of people from all over the country to participate and show their support for religion and their disdain for communism. The very same day, General Secretary Urbanek agreed to meet and talk for the first time with representatives of Civic Forum.

The Christian Church Today

While church attendance is up since the fall of communism and more young people seem to be coming back to the faith of their grandparents, many leading Catholics and Protestants are concerned that the church is not taking a stronger stand in social and economic issues that affect the new nation. One of the leading spokesmen for this point of view is Jakub Trojan, dean of the Protestant theological faculty at Charles University in Prague, who has written:

> Among the first tasks in the field of theology in my country . . . is overcoming the ghetto mentality that both the churches and theology adopted under the communist regime. . . . Today's Catholic theology and mission basically picks up where it left off—say, 40 years ago—as if nothing significant had happened morally and spiritually in the

meantime. Perhaps even more troublesome, it picks up as if important moral and spiritual forces had not changed the face of society *before* communism came to power in our region. Secularization was not invented and set in motion by the communists alone.

Trojan and other church leaders call for the Catholic and Protestant churches to recommit themselves in the political arena—ensuring that the poor and needy won't be left out of a competitive market economy and that environmental issues will be addressed in the Czech Republic.

The Czech Brethren

Among the oldest Protestant denominations in the Czech Republic is the Czech Brethren, also known as the Unity of Brethren and the Moravian Church. This church was founded by followers of Jan Hus in 1457 in Kunwald, Bohemia. Originally a radical religious group opposed to the abuses of the Catholic Church, the Brethren gradually grew more conservative and attracted a wider range of followers. By the 1520s, it had between 150,000 and 200,000 members in 400 congregations in Bohemia and Moravia. Strongly nationalistic, the Brethren developed in the late 1500s the six-volume Kralitz Bible, the first Bible written in the Czech language. Along with other Protestant churches, the Brethren was persecuted by the Catholics when the Czech lands faced defeat after the Battle of the White Mountain. Ministers continued to hold services secretly and many members fled to Germany, England and the United States. Here, they set up their own fully independent "settlement congregations." In 1982, the membership of the Brethren worldwide was 457,523.

The Jews

During World War II, The Jews of Czechoslovakia, like those in so many Eastern European countries, were rounded up and exterminated in concentration camps. Of those who survived, many never returned but resettled elsewhere. The Jewish ghetto in Prague is remarkably preserved today, with six synagogues still standing. One of them, Alt-Neu, dates back to the 11th century. But there are no Jews in the ghetto, although about 15,000 of them live in other parts of the city. Jewish tourists, descendants of those who lived and died here, can be found visiting Prague's old Jewish Cemetery, as observed here by travel writer Michael Chabon:

> The Old Jewish Cemetery was on this gray October afternoon filled with German tourists shuffling politely among the graves, their expressions mild and illegible. They called out one another's names, stooped to run their hands over the Hebrew inscriptions and left behind their unimaginable wishes, scrawled onto scraps of paper. This custom is an odd permutation of the traditional leaving of a stone at a Jewish graveside—unique, in my experience, to the old Prague

The Legend of the Golem

Some 300 years before Mary Shelley dreamed up Dr. Victor Franken-stein and his creation in an Italian villa, the Czechs had their own manmade monster—one that is inextricably linked to the Jews of Prague and their long history of persecution. According to the 16th-century legend, Rabbi Jehuda Low ben Bezalel of Prague (1520–1609) brought to life a life-size clay statue by putting a piece of paper in its mouth with the Hebrew word for *God* written on it. Low called his creature the *Golem,* Hebrew for a shapeless mass, and ordered it to protect the Jews of Prague from an evil emperor. The Golem, however, soon turned on the Jews as well and had to be destroyed.

The Golem legend has been retold time and again in literature and film. A German silent movie *Der Golem* (1914), which set the story in 20th century Prague, was directed by Henrik Galeen and Paul Wegener, who also played the Golem. The film was so successful that the two men remade it six years later. This version, which retold the original legend, was photographed by Karl Freund, who later came to Hollywood and directed such horror classics as *The Mummy,* starring Boris Karloff.

In the climax of the second Golem film, the monster murders a man and sets the Jewish ghetto on fire. The Jews and the city are saved by a little girl who befriends the creature and inadvertently removes the magic word from an amulet around its neck. The Golem instantly turns back into a lifeless statue. The striking style of this classic silent film had a direct influence on the famous Hollywood film *Frankenstein* that appeared 11 years later.

cemetery, where people use bits of rock, pebbles and even their pocket change to weigh down their written supplications, or cram their messages into the cracks in the weathered old tombs.

Although organized religion has been dealt serious blows in the 20th century in Czechoslovakia, it continues to be important for many Czechs today. In May 1995, Pope John Paul II briefly visited the Czech Republic. Part of his mission was to bring Protestants and Catholics closer together in a country where in the past they have often been in conflict: "I come as a pilgrim of peace and love," he proclaimed. In the city of Olomouc the pope canonized a local priest, Rev. Jan Sarkander, who was tortured to death by Protestants in 1620. The canonization, however, was a matter of controversy for some Protestants who considered Sarkander a traitor to Czech nationalism. The flaring up of old religious rivalries may be strangely comforting to religious Czechs, when so many of their compatriots seem indifferent to matters of religion, and yet there is a renewed sense of spirituality that many people have experienced since the triumphant events of 1989–90. President Havel, himself a lapsed Catholic, expresses what many Czechs must feel:

> I have certainly not become a practicing Catholic: I don't go to church regularly, I haven't been to confession since childhood, I don't pray, and I don't cross myself when I *am* in Church. . . . [However] there is a great mystery above me which is the focus of all men and the highest moral authority . . . that in my own life I am reaching for something that goes far beyond me and the horizon of the world that I know, that in everything I do I touch eternity in a strange way.

NOTES

p. 55   ". . . The endless, unchanging wasteland . . ." Václav Havel, *Disturbing the Peace* (New York: Knopf, 1990), pp. 184–85.

p. 57   "The church here is not . . . " Gale Stokes, *The Walls Came Tumbling Down: The Collapse of Communism in Eastern Europe* (New York: Oxford University Press, 1993), p. 152.

pp. 57–58 "Among the first tasks . . . " Jakub Trojan, "Theology and economics in the postcommunist era," *Christian Century,* March 16, 1994, p. 278.

pp. 59–60 "The Old Jewish Cemetery . . . " Michael Chabon, "Prague: Lost Era's Last Survivor," in *The Sunday New York Times,* Travel Section, September 26, 1993.

p. 60   "I come as a pilgrim . . . " *The Connecticut Post,* May 21, 1995.

p. 60   "I have certainly . . . " Václav Havel, *Disturbing the Peace,* p. 189.

7

The Economy

*H*istorically, the Czech economy has been one of the most active and robust in Europe. In the 19th century, while other Eastern European economies were still based on subsistence agriculture, the Czechs were mining coal and building factories. When Czechoslovakia was formed as a nation in 1918, it was considered one of Europe's leading industrial nations. The ravages of World War II and the subsequent takeover by the Communists changed all that.

The Economy Under Communism

When the Communists took industry and farming out of the hands of the individual and gave it to the state, they took away much of the incentive of Czechoslovakia's skilled workers and craftspeople. The Czechs prided themselves on their world-renowned light industries. The Communists shifted the emphasis to heavy industry—machinery and steel. Production of glassware and other consumer products was severely cut back. The state-run factories turned out shoddy products that Czech workers were ashamed to be associated with. The standard of living under the planned economy of the Soviets declined sharply.

The frustration faced by conscientious workers under the Soviet system is graphically depicted in this anecdote told by Czech president Havel, recalling the year he worked in a Trutnov brewery in 1974:

> . . . My immediate superior was a certain S, a person well versed in the art of making beer. He was proud of his profession and he wanted our brewery to brew good beer. He spent almost all his time at work, continually thinking up improvements. . . . The brewery itself was managed by people who understood their work less and were less fond of it, but who were politically more influential. They were bringing the brewery to ruin and not only did they fail to react to any of S's suggestions, but they actually became increasingly hostile toward him and tried in every way to thwart his efforts to do a good job. Eventually the situation became so bad that S felt compelled to write a lengthy letter to the manager's superior, in which he attempted to analyze the brewery's difficulties. He explained why it was the worst in the district and pointed to those responsible. . . . The manager of the brewery, who was a member of the Communist Party's district committee, had friends in higher places and he saw to it that the situation was resolved in his favor. S's analysis was described as a "defamatory document" and himself was labeled as a "political saboteur." He was thrown out of the brewery and shifted to another one where he was given a job requiring no skill. . . . He could now say anything he wanted, but he could never, as a matter of principle, expect to be heard. He had become the "dissident" of the Eastern Bohemian Brewery.

With the fall of communism the Czech economy has sprung back with a vengeance. There are today more than 2,000 private companies in the Czech Republic with a total value of $20.7 billion; they are responsible for 60 percent of national production. Unemployment in June 1993 was 2.63 percent, one of the lowest in Europe. In 1993, the government reported a small surplus. Trade with Germany and other Western countries is strong and rapidly expanding. Of all the nations in transition in Eastern Europe, none has experienced the consistent growth and economic benefits of the Czech Republic.

The present economy is a result of the way that the Czechs have managed to make good use of their resources.

Czech Industry—From Armaments to Breweries

Czech industry is highly skilled, and workers have a reputation for turning out top-quality, sophisticated products. Western and northern Bohemia is the center of Czech industry; here are manufactured everything from tractors to precision microscopes. Czech cut glassware has been made in northern Bohemia since the 1600s and is treasured around the world; even older are the fine breweries of Pilsen and other Bohemian cities and towns,

Brewing Beer: A Czech Tradition

"No one 'manufactures' great beer," says Václav Janouskovec, a foreman at the Pilsner Urquell brewery. "Brewing is a precision craft."

Pilsner Urquell, the oldest brewery in Pilsen, was founded in 1842. Its then-new technology revolutionized the brewing of beer in Europe. (Cedok Tours)

(continued on next page)

breweries that date back to the Middle Ages [see boxed feature]. Pilsen is so closely associated with the production of beer that *pilsner,* the lager bottled beer made here, has become the name for any lager beer with a strong hops flavor. Today, the Czech Republic is the sixth-largest producer of beer in the world.

A more recent industry is armaments, centered in the city of Brno. The famous Bren automatic gun used in World War II was invented here and later made in Enfield, England. Tanks and armored cars are also produced in Brno.

The chemical industry is another major area of the Czech economy, and plants are found in Prague, Brno and other cities. Chemists make plastics, paint, medicines and other products out of the raw materials of coal and oil.

He should know. His brewery, the oldest in the Czech Republic, has been practicing that craft for more than 150 years. Brewing beer in Bohemia goes as far back as the 10th century. In 1295, the town of Pilsen was granted a royal charter that gave 260 families the right to brew beer. This eventually led to a bitter dispute in the 16th century between the nobility and the common people, who wanted the right to brew beer, too. The conflict nearly led to civil war.

The brewing at Pilsner Urquell established a new technology in the 1840s that has since become a Bohemian tradition. Barley malt is mixed with grain and pure water that has been brought up from deep wells. The mixture is heated, and the starch in the grain is transformed into sugar. Carefully selected hops—the dried cones of the flower of a certain plant—are added to the brew to give it the distinctive flavor of Pilsner beer. The hops-rich brew is simmered in sixteen 6,500-gallon copper kettles in the boiling room. Next, yeast is added to start the fermentation process that turns the sugar into alcohol. The fermenting beer is poured into oak casks, where it ages for weeks or even months.

Finally, the finished lager beer is poured into tank trucks that deliver it to pubs and restaurants across the Czech Republic. Bottled Pilsner is shipped around the world.

When Czechs drink a pint of their golden, bubbly beer, they are keeping alive a tradition that goes back a thousand years.

The Czech Republic is famous for its finely crafted glassware. This young woman is cutting facets in lead crystal at a glass factory in Novy Bor. The work is pain-staking and dangerous because workers do not wear goggles and the room is poorly ventilated. (Thor Swift/Impact Visuals)

Heavy industry, developed by the Communists, includes steel plants located in Kaldno. The Czechs also manufacture cars, trucks, transportation equipment and heavy machinery.

Natural Resources

The fertile river-fed valleys of north-central Bohemia and central Moravia produce a variety of crops such as corn, rye, wheat, barley and sugar beets, from which sugar is extracted. Fruit trees in Moravia and Silesia produce apples, pears and plums, while strawberries and currants thrive in central Bohemia. Never ones to waste anything, the efficient Czech farmers store the overripe fruit in vats, where they are distilled for brandy and liqueurs. Poppy seeds are shaken by hand from the fried poppy heads and stored in boxes. They are used to decorate breads and cakes.

Forests cover 35 percent of the land. The largest is the great Bohemian Forest in the south. Lumbering is a major industry, and every tree has its particular uses: Conifers are used to build furniture and houses; beech and oak are the raw material for the many barrels, kegs and vats used in the Bohemian breweries; softer woods are used to make musical instruments, particularly church organs; pine resin or sap is an important ingredient in glues, varnishes and some medicines.

Mining was the first major industry in the Czech lands. The rich coal deposits of Bohemia and Silesia were first mined in the mid-19th century. Today, the Czech Republic is the seventh-largest coal producer in the world. Other minerals found in Bohemia include copper, gold, zinc, silver, uranium and iron ore. Silesia has deposits of magnetite.

The Czech Strategy— Avoid the Pain

While in Poland and elsewhere in Eastern Europe new governments have plunged forward toward a free-market economy and have experienced the pain of change and growth, the Czechs have taken a somewhat easier road. While many state-run businesses have been privatized, the Czechs have cushioned the shock of shifting to a free-market economy by continuing to provide government assistance in the form of subsidies to failing businesses and holding tight control over such expenses as rent for housing and utility bills. Those state industries that remain have been allowed to operate despite financial failure by the government in order to prevent job losses.

"The Czech strategy is creating admirable stability, but they haven't paid the whole price for it yet," observed Jan Vanos, president of Plan Econ, an economic consulting firm in the Czech Republic. "The Poles and the Hungarians are further along in the clean-up process. The upheaval in the Czech Republic may not be as bad as in other countries, but the Czechs are still going to have to take some hits."

For some workers the "hits" have already begun. The formerly state-owned Poldi Kladno steel mill near Prague has had to cut its work force more than half as more-efficient Western production has taken away much of its business. Although the government has helped many workers find new jobs in Prague and other cities, a number of them are making less money than they did before. "So far the economic reforms have really hurt my standard of living," confessed one 50-year-old plant worker. "But every new beginning is difficult. If not me, then my children and grandchildren will see better times."

This positive attitude may help many Czechs get through some of the rough days ahead, although similar difficulties faced by the Poles and Hungarians have caused them to look to ex-Communist leaders for a slightly slower and less bumpy road to capitalism.

The American Invasion and Local Entrepreneurs

Once relying mostly on the Soviet bloc for as much as 70 percent of its trade, today the Czech Republic has made tremendous strides in trading with the Western nations. In 1993, trade with Western Europe shot up 16 percent. Much of this trade is with its neighbor to the west, Germany. In its strategic location between Eastern and Western Europe, the Czech Republic may become the main conduit for trade between these two regions.

At the same time, many foreign businesses are opening stores and shops in the Czech Republic. Among them is the American cosmetic firm Estée Lauder. The Lauder Prague store so far has had few customers able to afford their products, but they, like other American and European businesses, are gambling on growth as the Czechs become more prosperous and have more money to spend on luxuries. "If you wait until there are enough people to support a big business, there'll be enough competition and the market will be carved up so it will be ten times more costly . . ." said company president Leonard A. Lauder. "We're prepared for several years of no profits because we know as the economy strengthens we'll be well positioned."

A line of employees await a crush of customers at the first McDonald's restaurant to open in Prague in April 1992. American companies and entrepreneurs flocked to the Czech Republic after communism's fall to take advantage of this new market for their products and services. (David Reed/Impact Visuals)

Established American businesses aren't the only ones anxious to make money in the Czech Republic. Since 1991, hundreds of young Americans, many fresh out of college, have flocked to Prague to enjoy the city's beauty and its low cost of living, while starting a successful business. Americans in their 20s and 30s own discos, copy centers, pizza restaurants and the first laundromat in Prague. While some stay on indefinitely, many leave in a year or less and return home.

"Money is going to be made by people who take risks," said Matthew Morgan, an American who runs a public-relations firm in Prague. "The Czechs don't know how to make money. They're not trying. They don't know that capitalism is based on hard work."

This condescending attitude and the fact that most of the Americans in Prague keep to themselves and contribute little to Czech society has had a negative effect. Many Czechs have grown tired of their "American cousins" and the materialism they represent. They are also learning how to "make money" and run their own businesses.

One outstanding example of a successful self-made Czech business-person is Ivana Juranova, who worked as a secretary for a newspaper before communism's fall. On her own, Juranova decided to start up her own business, selling ad space for clients: "All of a sudden I was in the kitchen with a telephone. My only software was a piece of paper and my brain." In a short time, she managed to parlay these assets into a $4.5-million company called Medea S.R.O.

This kind of success story is very satisfying to Prime Minister Václav Klaus, who has largely engineered the nation's economic plan. "Three years ago my two sons, at the time 21 and 16, had never in their lives entered a private grocery shop, butcher shop, hairdresser," he explained. "Today, within a mile of where we live, there probably is not one state-owned shop, cafe or service."

As the Czech Republic's transition to a full market economy continues, there will inevitably be bumps and detours in the road ahead. Yet, for the long haul, it looks as if it will arrive safely at its destination—economic independence and prosperity.

As one steel worker put it simply: "People know how to work in our country."

NOTES

p. 62   ". . . My immediate superior . . . " Václav Havel, *Open Letters: Selected Writings 1965–1990,* (New York: Knopf, 1991), pp. 173–74.

p. 63   "No one 'manufactures' . . . " Thomas J. Abercrombie, "Czechoslovakia: The Velvet Divorce," *National Geographic,* September 1993, p. 21.

p. 66   "The Czech strategy . . . " *The New York Times,* October 17, 1993.

p. 67   "So far the economic reforms . . . " *The New York Times,* October 17, 1993.

p. 67   "If you wait . . . " *The New York Times,* October 11, 1994.

p. 68   "Money is going to be made . . . " *The New York Times,* October 3, 1992.

p. 69   "All of a sudden . . . " Richard C. Morais, "Hong Kong of Europe," *Forbes,* June 20, 1994, p. 69.

p. 69   "Three years ago . . . " Richard C. Morais, *Forbes,* p. 69.

p. 69   "People know how . . . " *The New York Times,* October 17, 1993.

8

Culture

*T*he culture of the Czech Republic is a fascinating mixture of age-old tradition and modern experimentation. The Czechs have managed to preserve much of what is precious in their past—folk music, art, dance and folklore—while exploring new ways of expression in the arts, particularly in the 20th century. This restless search for innovation is characteristic of much of the best of Czech culture.

Language

The Czech language is a Western Slavic language, closely related to Polish, Serb and Slovak. Its 34-letter alphabet is loaded with consonants and has very few vowels. This gives spoken Czech a distinctly strange sound to foreigners. A favorite pastime among Czech intellectuals is creating sentences that don't contain a single vowel. Written accents are found in many Czech words, especially proper nouns, but the stress is always on the first syllable.

Historically, the Czech language has had its ups and downs. It remained largely a spoken language until Charles IV made it the official language of Bohemia's government, law and literature in the 14th century. In the 15th century, Jan Hus reinforced its importance when he preached in Czech to the people of Prague, foregoing German, still the dominant language of the church in his day. Hus also reformed and simplified Czech spelling in his written works.

With the defeat of the Czechs at the Battle of the White Mountain in 1620, the Hapsburgs of the Austrian Empire suppressed their language ruthlessly, realizing all too well its close connection with Czech nationalism. Jesuit priests, in league with the empire, burned entire libraries of Czech books, many of them priceless. By the middle of the 18th century, the Czech language was spoken primarily by peasants in the countryside. All educated people spoke German, the language of their Austrian rulers. Only with the dawn of the national movement in the early 19th century did Czech

The Czech people express their creativity in every aspect of their lives. These beehives in Roznov pod Radhostem, enlivened by folk art, are part of the oldest and largest Czech open-air museum, founded in 1925.
(Cedok Tours)

again become the language of all citizens—a symbol of their spirit and desire for independence. New dictionaries and grammars appeared and the language received its final codification late in the century in the ground-breaking work of Professor Jan Gebauer of the Czech University in Prague.

Today, Czech is spoken by about 10 million people—9 million in the Czech Republic and Slovakia and another million in the United States.

Literature

The earliest literature of Bohemia was church hymns, religious histories and poetic romances. All of these were written in Latin. Czech literature and language flourished during the Renaissance period, but the subjection of the Czechs by the Austrians was a terrible blow to the country's literary life. A reawakened nationalism, spearheaded by historian and intellectual Frantisek Palacký (1798–1876) in the 19th century, led to a flowering of Romantic patriotic literature. One of the finest of these writers was Karll Hynek Mácha (1810–36), whose epic poem *May*, published the year he died, is considered the finest poem in the Czech language. Mácha's verse was characterized by its melancholy mood and deep love of nature.

As the 19th century progressed, naturalism came to dominate Czech literature, as it did elsewhere in Europe. After the cataclysm of World War I, Czech literature became the finest and most exciting in Europe, due largely to three writers—Franz Kafka (see boxed biography), Karel Capek, and Jaroslav Hasek. Kafka's tales and novels of modern man's alienation from the world around him were among the most influential works in modern literature. But Capek (1890–1938) had a more immediate impact in his lifetime. In his plays and novels, Capek used science fiction and fantasy to express his moral and political ideas. In *R.U.R.* (1921), his most popular play, Capek created a race of mechanical men he called "robots," a word he invented from the Czech word *robota*, meaning "hard labor" or "servitude." In his novel *The Absolute at Large* (1922), Capek predicted the use of atomic energy. Along with his brother and frequent collaborator Josef (1887–1945), Capek also foresaw the rise of nazism, but his efforts to warn his fellow Czechs of its threat was to little avail. Three months after his death from inflammation of the lungs, German soldiers marched into Prague and took over the country. The Nazi secret police, the Gestapo, came to Capek's home to arrest him, unaware that he was already dead. Josef died six years later in a concentration camp shortly before the war ended.

Few novels have satirized war as effectively as *The Good Soldier Schweik* by Jaroslav Hasek (1883–1923). In this four-volume epic tale that remained unfinished at Hasek's death, Schweik, a good-natured dogcatcher, is drafted into the Austrian army during World War I and has numerous outrageous adventures. The novel proved so popular that German playwright Bertolt Brecht wrote a sequel in 1945, continuing Schweik's adventures into World War II.

After the Communists took over Czechoslovakia in 1948, it became, in the words of German novelist Heinrich Böll (1917–85), a "cultural cemetery." Censorship and an emphasis on social realism, a literary style that mainly served as propaganda for the Communists, kept writers from expressing their true feelings and thoughts. The works of Kafka and other older Czech writers were banned.

Censorship was loosened in the 1960s, and a new generation of writers emerged who used the dark, surreal humor of their predecessors to express their disillusionment with the Communist system. In his plays, Václav Havel used absurd comedy and language to satirize the soulless bureaucracy of the Communist system mercilessly. "Like Eugène Ionesco [1912–1994], he is deeply concerned with language and the possibility of meaningful communication," wrote one critic. " . . . He is specifically concerned with the fate of language threatened by the meaningless slogans of a communist bureaucracy."

With the increasing politicizing of writers and intellectuals in the 1970s and the formation of Charter 77 in 1977, many people employed in the arts became targets of persecution for the government. They lost jobs, had their works banned and were forced, like Havel, to take demeaning jobs to survive economically.

On a trip to Prague in the early 1980s, American writer Philip Roth (1933–) was struck with the absurdity of this situation:

> . . . The workmen at their beer [in the restaurant] reminded me of Bolotha, a janitor in a museum now that he no longer runs his theater. "This," Bolotha explains, "is the way we arrange things now. The

Franz Kafka (1883–1924)

A young traveling salesman wakes up one morning to find that he has been transformed into a gigantic insect. A bank assessor is accused of a crime that he has no knowledge of committing; he is tried, eventually convicted and executed. An official in a penal colony demonstrates an ingenious torture machine to a visitor; when it becomes apparent that the machine will be

Franz Kafka's fiction was so anxiety-ridden that it gave a new word to the English language—Kafkaesque—that is used to describe anything that is bizarre or nightmarish. (The New York Public Library Picture Collection)

menial work is done by the writers and the teachers and the construction engineers, and the construction is run by the drunks and the crooks. Half a million people have been fired from their jobs. *Everything* is run by the drunks and the crooks. They get along better with the Russians." . . . I look at the filthy floor and see myself sweeping it.

Despite the restrictions on their work under communism, some Czech writers were greeted with great critical acclaim abroad, including the novelist Milan Kundera (1929–) and the poet Jaroslav Seifert (1901–86), who won the Nobel Prize in literature in 1984.

Today, in the post-Communist era, Czech writers are free once again to express themselves, and book publishing is a flourishing business.

outlawed by the colony's commandant, the official attaches himself to the machine and dies horribly.

These are three of the plots created by the dark imagination of Franz Kafka, one of the most extraordinary and influential writers of the 20th century. Kafka's life was as drab and unhappy as his novels and tales were bizarre. He was born in Prague into a middle-class Jewish family that spoke German. A troubled, sensitive young man, he studied law and then worked most of his adult life as a state insurance lawyer for the government. He wrote in his spare time and published only a few stories in his lifetime.

Kafka's fiction explores the relationship of the human being to society and God and the human's utter alienation from both. Although he often describes unreal and fantastical events, Kafka's cool, precise prose lends them the clear reality of a dream. The cruelty of life and humanity's frustrated search for meaning and salvation as depicted in his novels *The Trial* (1925) and *The Castle* (1926), foreshadow the rise of Nazi Germany, the concentration camps and the deadening bureaucracy of communism. Kafka died of tuberculosis at age 41. In his will, he named what he considered his best books and wrote that "Should they disappear altogether that would please me best. . . . But everything else of mine [including his three novels] . . . without exception is to be burned, and I beg you to do this as soon as possible." Fortunately for world literature, his executor and friend, Max Brod, ignored the will, edited Kafka's novels and found a publisher for them.

Music

The folk music of Bohemia has had a profound influence on the great classical Czech composers, whose music is played and revered today. Bedrich Smetana (1824–84) used folk songs and dances in his great comic opera *The Bartered Bride* (1866) and other works. Antonín Dvorák (see boxed biography) continued Smetana's tradition and borrowed brilliantly from Czech and Slovak folk music in his *Slavonic Dances,* the work that first brought him to international attention.

Leos Janácek (1854–1928) brought Czech music boldly into the 20th century with a series of ground-breaking operas. Although he had written many outstanding orchestral and choral works, it was not until a Prague production of his opera *Jenufa* in 1916 that Janácek, at age 60, was hailed as a major composer. In his often tragic operas, Janácek used human speech as a dramatic element in his music and explored extremely complex psychological states of mind in a way opera had not done before.

Prague has been a musical capital of Europe going back to the time of Mozart. That great composer wrote his comic opera *Don Giovanni* as a commission for the city's Tyl Theater and conducted the first performance of it there himself in 1787. The Czech National Orchestra continues to perform the works of Mozart and other great composers, and an annual spring music festival in Prague is one of Europe's musical highlights.

Antonín Dvorák (1841–1904)

The first Czech composer to gain international recognition, Dvorák's best-known work was composed and written as a tribute to the United States. Dvorák was born in Helahozevis, a village near Prague, where his father was an innkeeper and butcher. He studied music at the Organ School in Prague and became a viola player in the Czech National Orchestra. His first important composition, the cantata *Hymnus*, was performed publicly in 1873.

The best known of Czech composers, Antonín Dvorák was a deeply religious and humble man. He composed his famous religious choral work, Stabat Mater *(1876), after the tragic death of two of his children.* (The New York Public Library Picture Collection)

Today, jazz music competes with folk and classical music in popularity in the Czech Republic. Jazz, although frowned on by the Communists, was one of the few art forms not banned following the crackdown after Prague Spring in 1968. "The communists beat up everybody, but jazz was sacrosanct to them because for some reason—maybe Lenin said so—jazz was considered the music of the proletariat [the working class]," said jazz pianist Morton Kratochvil in an interview.

Within a decade of its founding in 1971, the Jazz Federation, a section of the Czech Musicians Union, had grown to include a membership of some 20,000 people. It had become the only independent body of its kind in Czechoslovakia. Although the Federation was responsible for the popular Prague Jazz Days, it took on an importance far beyond jazz. The

Two years later, he met German composer Johannes Brahms (1833–97), who would become a close friend and mentor. Through Brahms, Dvořák found a publisher for his first set of *Slavonic Dances* (1878), which brought him instant fame. His other works include chamber works for small musical groups, songs, choral works, operas and nine symphonies.

In 1892, Dvořák, now a professor of musical composition at the Prague Conservatory, was invited to come to America and be director of the new National Conservatory of Music in New York City. He accepted the offer and spent three years in the United States, during which he wrote his most popular work, the Symphony *from the New World* (1893). The symphony is filled with magnificent melodies and the restless, nervous energy so characteristic of Dvořák's work. Many listeners believed that the composer incorporated Negro spirituals and Native American themes into his music. Dvořák later denied that he had done so, but he also wrote, "I am satisfied that the future music of this country must be founded upon what are called the Negro melodies. . . . These beautiful and varied themes are the product of the soil. . . . They are the folksongs of America, and your composers must turn to them. All the great musicians have borrowed from the songs of the common people."

Homesick, Dvořák returned to his beloved Prague in 1895 and died there from a stroke of apoplexy nine years later.

word *jazz* itself came to mean not just a certain kind of music but, in the words of the Federation, "a symbol of creativity, humanity and tolerance." Writers, artists and musicians and composers of every style of music were members. The Communist government saw the Federation as a threat to its authority and started a systematic campaign of harassment and defamation. It withdrew the permit allowing the organization to hold the Prague Jazz Days, which had grown into an international festival featuring not only jazz but rock and other avant-garde music. In 1984, the government banned the Czech Musicians Union from all activities and three years later arrested seven members of the Jazz Federation, charging them with "authorized banned activities." In a trial that gained great attention in the West, five of the seven were found guilty, but only two served short prison terms. The Soviet policy of glasnost had made the Czech government move more leniently than they might have otherwise.

In the post-Communist Czech Republic, jazz is more popular than ever. Jazz artist Kratochvil is a major entrepreneur whose company is not only involved in the record business, but also video, film, radio and real estate.

Art

As in literature and music, the first Czech art was religious, and included paintings, stained-glass windows, statues and tapestries going back a thousand years. In later centuries, Western art had a strong influence on Czech painting, sculpture and architecture. Many fine examples of the 17th-century baroque exist today in the nation's elaborate castles and churches.

The literate blandness of social realism deadened Czech art in the 1950s and 1960s, but Czech artists did their part to resist. In 1984, graphic designer Joska Skalnik devised a way that artists unrecognized by the government could "exhibit" their work. He invited some 300 Czech and Slovak artists to create works that could be contained within a small, lidless wooden box. Nearly three-quarters of them responded. Skalnik hid the boxes in a shed on the outskirts of Prague, where they remained until the collapse of the Communist government five years later.

Since then, these remarkable works have been seen in the United States and other countries. The range and expressiveness of these "mini-salon boxes" are extraordinary. One, by artist Jiri Stamfest, shows four tiny dolls running down a flight of stairs against a blank wall. Other artists fought against the repression that they felt the box represented. "I felt I had to change it rather than create something in it," said Margita Titlova. "I made a fire out in the countryside and placed the box on it upside down." The fire, which burned a hole in the back of the box, "is like revolutionary action," she added. In 1993, the Czech government proclaimed the boxed art a national treasure.

Theater

The theater has been a vital part of Czech life from the religious plays of the early Catholic Church to the biting satires of Havel and other playwrights during the Communist regime. The theater has rarely been an elitist art form, but one that Czechs of all classes have enjoyed. When the National Theater opened in Prague in 1883, the money to build it came from the donations of Czechs from every walk of life.

Despite the popularity of folk plays and realistic dramas of village life in the last century, Czech drama has most often been a theater of ideas. The great Moravian bishop, scholar and educator, Jan Ámos Komenský (1592–1670), usually referred to by the Latinization of his name, Comenius, was also an accomplished playwright. He used drama to give voice to his thoughts and philosophy on education and other contemporary issues. In the 1920s and 1930s, the Capek brothers, as noted, expressed their critique of modern technological society through their plays. In the pre– and post–World War II years, the Liberated Theater Company of Prague featured anti-Fascist revues performed by the renowned clown team of Voskovec and Werich. The ABC Theater, home of this famous troupe, was where Václav Havel's first satirical plays were produced.

One of the most popular forms of theater in the Czech Republic is puppetry. Puppet theaters have a long and honored tradition in Bohemia going back to the 17th century. The art of making puppets and marionettes and performing with them was handed down from father to son for

The arts have held a premier place in the life of Prague since the days of Charles IV. A full house watches a play being performed at the dazzlingly ornate National Theater. (Cedok Tours)

generations. Professional puppet theaters abound in Prague and other cities and offer fare ranging from Shakespearean-style plays to fairy tales and contemporary satire. One of the best-known and most intriguing puppet theaters is Prague's Spejbl and Hurvinek Theater, founded in 1945 by Josep Skupa. Spejbl and Hurvinek are father and son marionettes, whose outrageous adventures are enchanted by projected visual images and colorful musical numbers. Today, the Czech theater remains, in the words of Havel, "the spiritual home of its time."

Film

For such a small country, the Czech Republic has made an extraordinary contribution to the art of the cinema. The first movies were shot here by amateur photographer Jan Krizenecky (1868–1921) in 1898 and the first permanent movie theater opened in Prague in 1907. With the formation of Czechoslovakia in 1918, movie production increased rapidly, and by 1922, 34 feature films were being produced annually.

Despite the censorship of the Communists after World War II, cinema flourished in Czechoslovakia with the establishment of a national film school, FAMU. The first director to achieve international fame was Jirí Trnka (1912–69), whose puppet animation brought to life surreal fantasies, often with a political point. The 1960s brought a new generation of young, innovative filmmakers to the fore, led by Milos Foreman (1932–) and Jirí Menzel (1938–). Foreman's *Loves of a Blonde* (1965) was a winning combination of gentle humor and improvisation. Menzel's *Closely Watched Trains* (1966), which won an Academy Award as Best Foreign Film, was a tragicomedy about a young Czech working in a country railway station in German-occupied Czechoslovakia during World War II. Both films were international hits. Foreman defected to the United States soon after the Soviet invasion of 1968. He has had great success with films that are particularly American, such as *One Flew Over the Cuckoo's Nest* (1975), for which he won an Oscar as Best Director, *Hair* (1979) and *Ragtime* (1982).

Czech cinema continues to challenge its audiences to think and feel. The long tradition of Czech animation continues in the work of Jan Svankmajer, who uses his strange blend of animation and marionettes and dolls to retell such classic stories as *Alice in Wonderland* and the Faust legend. One *New York Times* critic praised his short films for "evoking Poe or Kafka, [and] bringing the menace of the subconscious to life."

"The main route by which society is inwardly enlarged, enriched and cultivated is that of coming to know itself in ever greater depth, range, and subtlety," wrote playwright and future president Václav Havel in an open letter to general secretary of the Czech Communist Party Dr. Gustav Husak in 1975. "The main instrument of society's self-knowledge is its culture: culture as a specific field of human activity, including the general state of mind—albeit often very indirectly—and at the same time continually subject to its influence."

Through freedom and repression, their culture has been a source of comfort and challenge to the Czechs and to the rest of us as well.

NOTES

p. 73   "cultural cemetery," *The Sunday New York Times Book Review,* December 10, 1989, p. 43.

p. 73   ". . . Like Eugène Ionesco . . . " William E. Harkins, in *The Reader's Encyclopedia of World Drama* (New York: Thomas Crowell, 1969), pp. 165–66.

p. 73   ". . . The workmen at their beer . . . " Phillip Roth, quoted in *Prague* (New York: Knopf, 1994), p. 120.

p. 75   "Should they disappear . . . " John Eastman, *The People's Almanac #2* (New York: Bantam, 1978), p. 1197.

p. 77   "The communists beat up . . . " Richard C. Morais, "Pioneer Entrepreneur," *Forbes,* June 20, 1994, p. 78.

p. 77   "I am satisfied . . . " Liner notes, recording of Dvořák's *Symphony No. 9 (From the New World),* performed by the Cleveland Orchestra, CBS's Great Performances series.

p. 78   "a symbol of creativity . . . " *Rolling Stone,* April 9, 1987.

p. 78   "authorized banned activities" *Rolling Stone,* April 9, 1987.

p. 79   "I felt I had to . . . " *The New York Times,* November 28, 1994.

p. 80   "the spirtual home . . . " Václav Havel, quoted in *Prague* (New York: Knopf, 1994), p. 55.

p. 81   "evoking Poe or Kafka . . . " *The New York Times,* October 26, 1994.

p. 81   "The main instrument . . . " Václav Havel, *Open Letters: Selected Writings, 1965–1990,* (New York: Knopf, 1991), p. 63.

9

Daily Life

---

*E*ven before the fall of communism, life in Czechoslovakia was easier than in most countries in Eastern Europe. The Czechs and Slovaks may have been more politically repressed than, for example, the people of Poland, but economically they were better off. Despite a shortage in housing and consumer goods, Czechoslovakia enjoyed one of the highest standards of living in the region. By the early 1980s, nearly one-fifth of Czech families owned cars. Many others owned such luxury items as television sets, telephones and refrigerators. Today, free of the drain that Slovakia put on the economy, the Czech Republic is doing better than ever. Life is generally good in this time of political and economic transition, but it is far from perfect.

" . . . Czechs regard their future with a mixture of hope, apprehension, and confusion," observes British writer Michael Ivory. "Some are embracing every aspect of Western culture, with unthinking admiration; others see old certainties crumbling and are only too ready to look for scapegoats."

The "embracers" are very evident in Prague, which has awakened after a long slumber of communism. The westernmost of the Eastern European countries, the Czech Republic has often in the past identified with the West. Now it is able to fulfill its dream of becoming a kind of America in Central Europe.

"The Czechs can't seem to explore fast enough all they missed out on during 40 years of communism," observed American Edmund White on a visit to Prague in the fall of 1994. "They're digging into their own prewar modernist heritage. They're keeping their bars open 24 hours a day, they're translating books from every language, and they're traveling as much as the disadvantageous exchange rate permits. The frantic desire to catch up accounts for much of the exuberance of this thrilling youthful city."

Yet under all the exuberance, some things remain the same. Not all American ideas have penetrated everyday Czech life. American feminism, for example, with its emphasis on equal pay for women, more job opportunities and an end to sexual harrassment, is not important to Czech women in general and they see it as damaging to relations between men and women. Yet women, performing the same job as men, earn only half their salary. This seems particularly paltry when the average take-home pay of all Czech workers is only $200 a month.

Much of the glitter and luxury that can be seen in stores in Prague and other cities are not within the reach of the average Czech. Such stores are frequented by the lucky Czechs who have succeeded in private business or the American entrepreneurs who have made a killing in the new consumer market.

A small but vocal minority has sought out scapegoats to pin the blame on for their problems. Gypsies, Vietnamese immigrants and other minorities (see Chapter 11) have been blamed for taking away jobs from native Czechs and spreading crime and other social problems. They have become the targets of such hate groups as the skinheads.

The Czech Republic has about 4,000 skinheads, more than any other European country except Hungary and Germany. As in these other countries, Czech skinheads have evolved a subculture with its own literature, music and antiforeigner, racist philosophy. Orlik, the leading skinhead band in the Czech Republic, has sold 120,000 copies of its first record album. Skinhead magazines, called "skinzines," preach a brand of racial hatred that is disturbingly similar to nazism and includes material from American hate groups such as the White Ayran Resistance.

The majority of Czechs, however, shun such extremism. They may be unhappy with their prime minister's austere economic program and disillusioned with their once heroic president, but they carry on. As they coexisted with communism, so they will manage to coexist with the transition to a more democratic way of life. "The Czechs aren't as mad as the Poles," points out journalist Lulos Beniak. "They know it's time to pay a price for what happened in the past. People know there is a lot to be done and will tighten their belts."

Perhaps one of the main reasons the Czechs look forward to the future with some confidence is because they are relatively well educated. Indeed, the Czech educational system is one of the finest in Europe.

Education

Education has been a major concern in the Czech lands since the Middle Ages. Moravian bishop Jan Ámos Komenský, noted in the previous chapter, is generally acknowledged as the father of Czech learning. Among the radical ideas that he promulgated is that teaching should be done in the student's native language and not Latin, that languages are best taught conversationally, and that education should be free, universal and available to both boys and girls. He also wrote one of the world's first picture books for children, *Orbis sensualium pictus* (*The Visible World*), in 1658, in which he emphasized contact with objects in a child's immediate environment as a way to relate learning to everyday life. Komenský's books on how to educate children formed the cornerstone of the Czech educational system.

Today, all Czech children must go to primary school from the ages of 6 to 15. The academic curriculum is rigorous. Students in sixth grade, for example, take as many as eight subjects in 45-minute classes. Because most Czech families have two working parents, most elementary students go to *dorgina* (day care) after school until their parents arrive home.

After they have completed their ninth year of schooling, about half of all children enter the work force, often beginning with a three-year apprentice program. The remaining students continue their education at the secondary level, the equivalent of our high school. Those who choose may go to technical school to learn a trade. At age 19, those students who qualify by examination may attend one of the six universities in the Czech Republic.

Sports and Recreation

A fit body is as important to the Czechs as an able mind; so physical exercise begins at an early age. During their summer vacation, many Czech children attend special holiday-camps in the mountains where they hike, camp and play team sports such as soccer, volleyball and handball. Soccer is the most popular team sport in the country, as it is in many European countries. Tennis is among the most popular individual sports. Under the Communists, there was a national tennis program that trained 30,000 players. Of these, the most renowned are semiretired world champion Martina Navratilova and Ivan Lendl, both of whom now live in the United States.

The sport with the longest tradition in the Czech Republic is gymnastics. Gymnastics clubs called *sokols* (*falcons* in Czech) were centers of physical activity where trainers instilled young gymnasts with a sense of patriotism as well as self-discipline. The *sokols* were an important part of the Slavic nationalistic movement that began in the mid-19th century. It was this spirit of nationhood that caused the Communists to abolish the *sokols* in 1948, although they continued to train gymnasts, the best of whom went on to compete in the Olympics.

As important as the Olympics in the Czech Republic is the Spartakiade, an eight-day national exercise competition held once every five years in Prague during the month of June. More than 70,000 competitors compete in gymnastics contests, dance performances and army drills that are watched by millions of Czechs and Slovaks.

Favorite winter sports are skiing and ice hockey, which after soccer is the Czech Republic's most popular sport. The progress of the teams of the Elite League, the Czech equivalent to the United States's National Hockey League, are followed avidly by sports' fans. The hockey team Slavia Praha made international sports headlines in early 1995 when they hired the youngest hockey player in professional hockey history—15-year-old Jan Hovacek. Putting a youth still in school in the rough-and-tumble

These boys are participating in the Spartakiade, an eight-day national exercise competition held once every five years in Prague. (Cedok Tours)

world of pro hockey was a controversial decision that many people opposed, although Hovacek was happy to be playing. "At first I was excited about all the attention, but then it started to annoy me," the 15-year-old said in one interview. "But you know, now I'm getting used to it."

Food and Drink

Czech food has benefited, as the country's culture in general has, from geography. Located at the crossroads of Europe, Czech cuisine has taken the best from a number of its neighbors—the spicy meat stew called goulash from Hungary, schnitzel (veal cutlet) from Austria, soured foods from Russia and sauerkraut and dumplings from Germany.

Dumplings are a national passion, and the Czechs make them every way imaginable. They stuff them with bacon or cheese and fill dessert dumplings with fruits, such as apricots and plums. Prague hams are among the finest in Europe, and the fish carp is a favorite dish at Christmas. Czech breads and pastries, often covered in poppy seeds, are hearty and delicious. Whatever they eat for dinner, the Czechs like to wash it down with a bottle or two of their native beverage—Pilsner beer.

Although Czech food is tasty, a tourist who only eats in restaurants may not appreciate its variety. Restaurant food in the Czech Republic has a uniformity that is a legacy of the Communist era. What dishes restaurants served was subject to the so-called "menu police." These food censors, still on patrol as of early 1994, see that every restaurant cooks its food,

From Castle to Castle

A favorite leisure pastime in the Czech Republic is castle hunting. With thousands of castles scattered across the countryside of Bohemia and Moravia, a devoted castle-lover could keep busy for a long, long time.

One of the most spectacular castles for visitors is Karlstejn Castle, southwest of Prague, which was built by Charles IV from 1348 to 1357. Erected on

For many centuries, castles were the homes of Czech nobility and protected villages and towns from invaders. Pictured here is Perstejn Castle.

especially the Czech national dish of roast pork, dumplings and sauer-kraut, the same way. If a cook wants to serve a new dish, he or she must submit it dutifully to the menu police. "They test the recipe for 30 days, and only then can approve it for general consumption," notes writer Peter C. Newman. "They seldom do so because they still feel dutybound by their official rule book, which doesn't permit an extra puff of pepper to alter basic proletarian tastes."

The Media

The Czechs are big readers who are very interested in what is going on in the world around them. The circulation rate of newspapers in the Czech

---

terraces of a limestone rock, it consists of numerous buildings. The most famous of these is the Big Tower; it contains the Chapel of the Holy Rood, which is the home of the imperial jewels, of holy relics of the saints and of the Czech Crown of St. Wenceslas, one of the most stunning pieces of Gothic goldsmithing in existence.

Also near Prague is Krivaklat Castle, located in the middle of a forest. The castle dates at least as far back as 1110 but is best known for its late-Gothic additions from the 15th century. Its Great Hall of the Royal Palace has a celebrated collection of statues and paintings from this period.

Further south and east of Prague is Cesky Sternbeck, one of Bohemia's best-preserved Gothic castles. Built on a narrow promontory above the River Sázava for defensive purposes, the castle is remarkable for being owned by only one noble family until the middle of the 20th century.

Moravia has castles, too. One of the most famous is Bouzov Castle, which served as the headquarters of the Teutonic knights for nearly two-and-a-half centuries. Its deep dungeons and torture chambers were admired by Nazi leader Heinrich Himmler, who turned the castle into his private retreat during the German occupation of World War II. Today, Bouzov Castle's rich atmosphere is often put to use as a movie set.

Filled with mementos of distant and recent history, the castles of the Czech Republic are true treasure houses of the past.

Republic is 368 per 1,000 people. The press, enjoying its new-found freedom after four decades of Communist censorship, is often highly critical of public officials. Their relationship with Prime Minister Václav Klaus is particularly prickly. "The media are always wrong," Klaus told an American interviewer. "You have to be happy when they spell your name right."

There is one public television and radio corporation in the Czech Republic, a nationwide private TV network and two radio networks. There are also local private stations. There is one television and radio for roughly every three persons in the country. The introduction of cable television in recent years has allowed Czechs the opportunity to view Western programming from Europe and America, a country they find particularly fascinating.

In 1995, Radio Free Europe and Radio Liberty, two American broadcasting stations that brought news from the West to Communist countries during the cold war, moved their operation from Munich, Germany, to Prague at the invitation of the Czech government. Housed in the former Czechoslovak Parliament building, the two stations transmit news and information in 19 languages to the republics of the former Soviet Union and Eastern Europe.

Holidays

Holidays are often a time when the Czechs can look back fondly on earlier times, when life was less complicated.

A good example is Christmas. The season begins with Svaty Mikalas Day (Saint Nicholas Day) on December 6. The Czechs love Christmas so much that they've set aside two days to celebrate it. December 25 and December 26 are known as First Christmas and Second Christmas, and both are state holidays.

Although Christmas trees are found in most Czech homes, they are a recent tradition. Much older is the custom of cutting cherry-tree branches and putting them in water in the kitchen at the beginning of the Advent season. The flowering cherry blossoms are a favorite Christmas decoration and are also a reminder that spring is only a few months away. The girl who picks the branch watches expectantly to see if the blossoms bloom on Christmas Eve. If they do, tradition says, she will happily marry before the new year is out.

Another Czech Christmas custom is the making of Nativity scenes, called "Bethlehems." These scenes, displayed in homes, are much more elaborate than the manger scenes in other countries and can sometimes include a whole village-full of extra characters. These "Bethlehems" are often precious works of art, lovingly carved out of wood or formed from bread dough that is then painted.

The Easter season is second only to Christmas in importance. On Palm Sunday, known as *Kvetna Nedele* in Czech, the Catholic priests bless and hand out to churchgoers pussy willows instead of the traditional palms. Later that day, farmers wave the willows over their fields to ensure a good

Czech girls in folk costumes make a doll called a baba *from the last sheaf of grain to be harvested. This is an integral part of the harvest festival called Obzinsky.* (Cedok Tours)

harvest. In some villages, even today, people place the willow branches on their roofs to protect their homes from fire.

Harvest time, once an important part of life in Bohemia, is actually celebrated twice there. Posviceni is the church consecration of the harvest, while Obzinsky is a secular celebration. During this joyous time, field-workers make a wreath out of ears of grain, corn and wildflowers, and a doll called a *baba* from the last sheaf of grain to be harvested. These two symbolic objects are placed in a wagon and pulled in a merry procession to the house of the landowner. The workers present the wreath to their employer, who shows gratitude for a good harvest by inviting them to a feast with dancing.

Two patriotic holidays are St. Wenceslas's (St. Václav's) Day on September 28, honoring the patron saint of the former Czechoslovakia, and Czechoslovak Liberation Day on May 9, commemorating the liberation of the nation at the end of World War II by the United States and Soviet armies.

NOTES

p. 83   "Czechs regard their future . . . " Michael Ivory, *Essential Czech Republic* (Lincolnwood, Ill.: Passport Books, 1994), p. 106.

p. 84   "The Czechs can't seem . . . " Edmund White, "Prague's new face," *Vogue,* September 1994, p. 352.

p. 85   "The Czechs aren't as mad . . . " *The New York Times,* March 2, 1995.

p. 87   "At first I was excited . . . " *The New York Times,* January 31, 1994.

p. 88   "They test the recipe . . . " Peter C. Newman, "The Czechs' rebirth and menu police," *Maclean's,* January 10, 1994, p. 24.

p. 90   "The media are always wrong . . . " Richard C. Morais, "Hong Kong of Europe," *Forbes,* June 20, 1994, p. 75.

10

The Cities and Towns

---

*T*he Czech Republic is a small country, and although its population is largely urban, most of its cities are small, too. Prague, the capital, is the only city with a population of more than a million people. No other city has more than 400,000 people. However, many Czech cities and towns have a rich history and cultural importance that belie their size.

Golden Prague

Zlata Praha—Golden Prague. It is a nickname that this grand city on the banks of the River Vltava in central Bohemia has richly earned. Of all the great capitals of Eastern Europe, Prague alone survived the catastrophes of the 20th century with its heritage intact. Its narrow, cobbled-stone streets, its age-old cathedrals, its artfully designed bridges—all remain, giving it a sense of history that few European cities can match.

There are other reasons why Prague is called golden. Some say it is the strange golden glow on its venerated buildings in the late afternoon sunlight. Others believe the nickname refers to the precious medieval paintings and their gold leaf—one of the city's greatest treasures. For still others, the gold of Prague is the mystical gold of the alchemists, those ambitious early scientists who tried to transform base metals into gold with a mixture of science and magic from the 13th to the 17th centuries. For them, Prague was their home base, made hospitable by King Rudolf II, the monarch who also encouraged the more substantial scientific contributions of astronomers Tycho Brahe and Johannes Keppler.

Whatever is golden about Prague, it is not a place for the casual tourist. It demands more than a quick glance. "Prague . . . remains today, a spiritual city," notes writer Patricia Hampl. " . . . It remains powerful, as if the landscape of a dream has been brought to life. It is not simply beautiful . . . the beauty is broken. And this draws the heart out of you to it. It is a city that demands relation."

The first settlements established where Prague now stands go back at least as far as the ninth century. King Wenceslas I of Bohemia established an important German settlement here in 1232 and it eventually became the capital of Bohemia. Under the loving care of Charles IV, Prague became one of Europe's finest cities. For three centuries, the emperors of the Holy Roman Empire resided there.

The Thirty Years' War began in Prague when Bohemian Protestants threw representatives of the Catholic emperor of Austria out a window of Hradcany Castle in 1618. It ended for the Czechs two years later with the shattering defeat at White Mountain just outside the city. Although Prague was under Austrian rule for the next three centuries, it remained a cultural capital during the 18th century and the heart of the Czech nationalism movement in the 19th century.

As the capital of the newly formed Czechoslovakia in 1918, Prague was a center of literature and the arts between the wars, nourishing such writers as Franz Kafka and the poet Rainer Maria Rilke (1875–1926). During World War II, the city and its people suffered greatly but were spared the devastation of major bombing.

Today, Prague is a tourists' city, attracting some 12 million visitors a year. The most popular attraction and most dominating structure in Prague is Hradcany Castle, a huge castle complex on Hradcany (literally, Castle Hill), built during Charles IV's reign. It was the residence of the Bohemian kings and more recently was home to Czechoslovakia's presidents. Next to the castle is the splendid Cathedral of St. Vitus, started in the 10th century and not finished until 1929. It contains the tombs of St. Wenceslas and many other Bohemian kings and emperors. Numerous other churches and palaces dot this area.

The Mala Strna (Lesser Town) is at the foot of the Hradcany and is the best-preserved part of old Prague. Cross the Charles Bridge, the most lovely of the city's 13 bridges, and you are in Stare Mesto (The Old Town), where lies the oldest part of Charles University, the Carolinum and the Gothic Old Town Hall with its famous clock containing the statues of the

Busy Wenceslas Square, actually a boulevard, lies in the heart of Prague. The statue is of King Wenceslas, whose pious character was immortalized in the Christmas carol "Good King Wenceslas." (The Bettmann Archive)

12 apostles, which move every hour. A dramatic monument to Jan Hus stands in Old Town Square.

While tourists stick to these well-known sights, there is much more to see in old Prague for the more adventurous visitor. " . . . Beyond these well-traversed areas, Prague has a wealth of cobbled alleyways, hidden squares with romantic statues, churches, galleries and museums," writes American correspondent Jane Perlez. "Often a 100-yard detour down a small lane will yield surprising vistas and glorious, intact architecture."

On the right bank of the river lies Prague's New Town, built mostly in the 19th century; here is the business center of the city. In the heart of New Town is Wenceslas Square, actually a wide boulevard bustling with shoppers and tourists who patronize its hotels, shops and restaurants. At one end of the square is the National Museum, in front of which stands the impressive statue of Good King Wenceslas. The square was the scene of the dramatic Czech resistance during the Soviet invasion in August 1968 and 21 years later saw the demonstrations that led communism to finally crumble.

The Communists left Prague, Europe's oldest survivor, less joyous. While the joy is returning these days, a certain pathos remains. "Prague has the special sadness of being the last of its kind . . ." writes one author. " . . . [It is] a whimsical, spooky and vainglorious town." And a golden one.

Busy Brno and Beer-Making Pilsen

Located in the southeast, Brno (population 391,000) is the Czech Republic's second-largest city and the capital of Moravia. A major industrial center, Brno is known as "the Manchester of Moravia" because of its many textile and spinning mills. In it is also manufactured everything from typewriters to turbines.

Brno has a long history, predating perhaps any other town or city in the Czech Republic. The limestone hills to the north of Brno contain caves where artifacts of prehistoric people have been discovered. More recently, Brno was the headquarters of French emperor Napoleon Bonaparte, who defeated the Russians and Austrians in "the battle of the three emperors" nearby at Austerlitz in 1805. Brno later became one of the Austrian Empire's most productive industrial towns. Some of Brno's finest landmarks are 13th-century Spiulank Castle, with its infamous torture chambers, and Masaryk University, founded in 1919.

Magical Waters: The Spas of Northern Bohemia

In northwest Bohemia are a group of small towns that for centuries have attracted the sick, the sluggish, the overweight and the well-to-do of Europe. They have come to this region to bathe in and drink from the medicinal mineral springs.

Perhaps the most famous of these spa resorts is Karlovy Vary (population 60,950, 1980 census), also known by its German name, Karlsbad. The town was officially chartered by King Charles IV in the 14th century. It was Charles who, according to legend, discovered its more than 60 restorative springs. Aristocrats and the famous, from Russia's Peter the Great to German author Johan von Goethe, have come to Karlovy Vary to relax and improve their health. The town is also known for its exquisite china and porcelain and an annual international film festival.

Nearby is Mariánské Lázne (population 17,932, 1980 census), often called Marienbad and referred to as "A pearl in the string of spas." Its curative spring and baths are located on the grounds of a 12th-century abbey. Among the resort's most celebrated visitors are Polish composer Frédéric Chopin and King Edward VII of England. Mariánské Lázne is also the site of a number of international congresses and conferences.

Equally renowned is tiny Jáchymov, whose earthly wealth includes not only its springs but mineral deposits of iron, radium, zinc and cobalt. Polish scientist Marie Curie (Manya Sklodowska) first discovered radium in its original metal state here. Jáchymov is also the most important pitchblende-mining center of Europe.

Centuries ago, Jáchymov was also known for its silver mines. A coin, called the *Jioachimsthler,* was first struck there in the 16th century. The name of the coin was shortened to *Thaler,* from which our word *dollar* is derived. Next time you spend a dollar, you might give a thought to the lovely old spas of the Czech Republic.

Pilsen (population 167,488) in western Bohemia is an industrial center too, lying near a rich deposit of coal fields. The Skoda Works, formerly known during the Communist era as the Lenin Works, produces armaments, automobiles and heavy machinery. But Pilsen is best known for its breweries that produce some of the best beer in the world.

Pilsen was founded in 1290 by King Wenceslas II, who turned it into a major trading town. During the nation's violent religious wars, Pilsen remained a Roman Catholic stronghold. Its splendid example of Renaissance and baroque architecture include the towering cathedral of St. Bartholomew that dominates the city's largest square. During World War II, the Nazis made Pilsen a leading producer of German weapons.

Industrial Ostrava and Historic Olomouc

Ostrava (population 331,000) in the northeastern corner of Moravia is the center of the most heavily industrialized region of the country. Coal mining is important here, as is the production of iron and steel and parts for bridges and ships.

A small town during the Middle Ages, Ostrava was critical because of its proximity to the Moravian Gate, the entrance to the lowlands. With the coming of the railroad in the 19th century, the city grew in size and population. Among its most famous institutions is a well-known college of mining and metallurgy.

Olomouc (population 107,000) in north central Moravia has a long and colorful past. Once the leading city of Moravia, Wenceslas II of Bohemia beat back the invading Mongols here in 1242. In 1469, Matthias Corvinus, king of Hungary, had himself crowned king of Bohemia in Olomouc. It was also here that Austria and Prussia signed the famous agreement in 1850 that dissolved the German Union and reinstated the German Confederation governed by Austria. Olomouc's infamous fortress, long gone, once imprisoned French statesman and soldier the marquis de Lafayette.

Olomouc is equally famous for its historic buildings—the Cathedral of St. Wenceslas and two Gothic churches—and the tasty candy and chocolate that it manufactures.

Towns—Large and Small

South of Prague, not far from the Austrian border, lies Ceské Budejovice (population 99,000) on the Vltava River. An important river port and rail

Karolvy Vary is the best known of the spa resorts of northern Bohemia. This thermal sanatorium pool is believed to cure numerous ills. (Cedok Tours)

and roadway center, the town is most famous for its breweries, some of the finest in Bohemia. Few Americans realize that Budweiser, the best-selling beer in the United States, is derived from Budvar, a beer made in Ceské Budejovice for the past 300 years. When not enjoying the local beer, visitors flock to the town's inner town with its quaint arcaded square that was built soon after Ceské Budejovice's founding in the 13th century.

Zlín (population 81,000) in central Moravia on the Drevnice River is known primarily for one thing—shoes. In 1913 Tomás Bat'a, a peasant shoemaker who had studied Henry Ford's assembly line in the United States, opened a shoe factory here. It eventually grew into a remarkably self-sufficient factory community. After World War II, the Communists nationalized the industry and renamed it Svit. The town underwent a name change, too: It was renamed Gottwaldov in honor of Klement Gottwald, the first Communist president of Czechoslovakia. It became Zlín again after the fall of communism.

Today, the shoe factory has been turned back over to the sons of Tomás Bat'a, and Zlín is one of the largest shoe-manufacturing centers in the world, producing 300,000 pairs a week. "We ship cows in one end, shoes out the other," explains factory spokesman Jaroslav Stokláska.

In the far west of the country, near the German border, lies tiny Cheb (population 26,051). A center of lignite mining, Cheb also produces machinery, watches and textiles. As a transportation center, it links the railroad with smaller towns such as Karlovy Vary, one of Europe's most popular health spas [see boxed feature]. A small Slavic settlement, Cheb was made part of Bohemia in 1322 by John of Luxembourg. The most memorable historic event that took place in Cheb was the murder of Bohemian general Albrecht Wallenstein, Czech leader in the Thirty Years' War. He was killed by his own generals in 1634 inside a 17th-century castle that still stands.

Historically rich, beautifully evocative and technologically advanced, the cities and towns of the Czech Republic are dramatic evidence of the country's past, present and future.

NOTES

p. 94   "Prague . . . remains today, . . . " Patricia Hampl, *A Romantic Education* (Boston: Houghton Mifflin, 1981), p. 211.

p. 96   ". . . Beyond these well-traversed areas, . . . " Jane Perlez, "What's Doing in Prague," *The Sunday New York Times*, Travel Section, August 28, 1994.

p. 96   "Prague has the special sadness . . . " Michael Chabon, "Prague: Lost Era's Last Survivor," *The Sunday New York Times*, Travel Section, September 26, 1993.

p. 100   "We ship cows . . . " Thomas J. Abercrombie, "Czechoslovakia: The Velvet Divorce," *National Geographic*, September, 1993, p. 20.

11

Present Problems and Future Solutions

*I*n his introduction to the collection of writings entitled *After the Velvet Revolution,* Tim Whipple relates an anecdote told around Prague on the eve of the fall of communism.

> The leaders of the Soviet Union, the United States and Czechoslovakia are each granted one question of God. Mikhail Gorbachev goes first. The Soviet leader wants to know what his country will be like in twenty years' time. "Capitalist," says God, at which Gorbachev collapses in tears. George Bush gloats and asks the same question about the United States, but God's reply is "Communist," whereupon Bush starts to wail as well. Undaunted Milos Jakes, general secretary of the Communist party, asks what the future holds for Czechoslovakia—and it's God who weeps, with pity.

> With the unimaginably rapid collapse of the Communist system in
> November and December [1989], God finally seemed to be cracking
> a wary smile over Czechoslovakia's future.

The smile that began in 1990 may now safely be described as more of
a grin, but one that could still turn into a grimace. The Czech Republic
has attained a high level of achievement in a very short time: it has the
lowest unemployment and lowest inflation in Eastern Europe, its government is the most stable in the region and its ability to attract Western trade
and commerce is the envy of its neighbors.

Most amazingly, it has achieved all this with a minimum of pain and
hardship for its people. This is not all to the good, however, say many
observers. The leaders of the Velvet Revolution have created a velvet
government that goes easy on everything, including the economy. The
pragmatic and creative Czechs have gone out of their way to avoid the
hard decisions that have been made in Poland and Hungary, where many
of the props that held up the welfare state have been removed. In the
Czech Republic, state subsidies and welfare programs are still in place to
cushion any discomfort in this difficult transitional phase. But these
programs will have to end if the economy is to become a truly free-market
one, and then some of the pain may hit home.

Class Structure and the Economy

Whatever the future may hold, the Czechs are experiencing some economic problems now, and they are not very different from those in
neighboring countries.

Where in 1989 there was one class of people struggling together in
Czechoslovakia, today two distinct classes are emerging in the new Czech
Republic—the few who have struck it rich from capitalism and the majority
who are still struggling to make it in a new and unfamiliar world. While
the average Czech has a higher standard of living than in any other Eastern
European country, the Czech worker still brings home the equivalent of
only $200 a month. The newly opened fancy shops and boutiques in
Prague and other cities are not for these wage earners.

The cold truth is that the lot of the average wage earner will probably not improve any too soon. Catching up with the Western economies could take decades, many economists now predict. Even to reach the standard of living of Spain, one of the poorer countries in Western Europe, could take a decade or more. While the majority waits for things to improve, the rich will continue to get richer, something that may create some political turmoil for the conservative government of Václav Klaus.

"We are experiencing cultural shock," said Jirina Siklova, a professor of sociology at Charles University. "New relationships among the social strata are just now forming. No one knows who will be poor tomorrow and who rich and the new or revamped code of moral and real values has not yet been universally accepted."

Solutions to these economic problems do exist, and some are being pursued. One is to encourage more Czech entrepreneurs by making capital more accessible to them. Money is so tight that those starting a business are often forced to bribe bank officers just to get a loan. By making money more available, banks and the government can stimulate both new businesses and the economy.

Anti-Americanism

When an American film crew came to Prague in the spring of 1995 to film *Mission Impossible,* the first major Hollywood movie ever made here, they had high expectations. Three weeks later, they left angry and disillusioned. The price to shoot the exterior of the famed Liechtenstein Palace had been raised from $2,000 to more than $23,000 a day, claimed the film's producer and star, Tom Cruise. "Our impression was they'd gone from communism to rabid capitalism without any mitigating force," said Katherine Orloff, the film's publicity agent. The Czech government, in turn, blamed the Americans for the misunderstanding, although President Havel defended the filmmakers, claiming use of the palace should have been given for free.

This new wave of anti-Americanism in the Czech Republic may be the direct result of the United States invasion of Prague that started in the early 1990s: The army of young, ambitious Americans who came to live and open businesses in Prague were at first welcomed with open arms by the

Czechs in America

There are about a million Czech-speaking people in the United States, more than in any other country outside the Czech Republic. Many Czechs came to this country after 1848, a year of turmoil and revolution in Europe. They settled mainly in the Midwest and Canada.

Although there are large Czech populations in New York City, Los Angeles and Newark, New Jersey, the city known as the "Czech Capital of America" is little Wilber, Nebraska, population 1,624, in the southeastern corner of the state. Every August, for one weekend, Wilber hosts the National Czech Festival and comes alive with folk dancing, music and an enormous amount of eating. Czech dishes such as roast duck, dumplings and sauerkraut are consumed in great quantities. There's even a contest to see who can eat the most *kolaches,* Czech sweet buns. On the second day of the festival, special awards are presented to those who have promoted Czech and Nebraskan culture.

Another small but thriving Czech community, Spillville, Iowa, made the great Czech composer Antonín Dvorák a little less homesick during the three years he lived in America. Dvorák spent his holidays at Spillville and completed his last symphony, *From the New World,* there.

Czech Americans have made valuable contributions to American life. Some of the most famous of them are actor Walter Slezak, Nobel Prize–winning biochemists Carl and Gerty Cori and business magnates Joseph Bulova (of wristwatch fame) and Ray Kroc, who turned MacDonald's and fast food into an American institution. When asked what was the secret of his success, Kroc invariably replied, "I am of Bohemian extraction, and I have always believed in hard work. . . ."

Czechs, but time changed their admiration to disillusionment. The Americans had taken and given back little in return. As one Czech student put it:

> We were so astonished at the appearance of live Americans. We said look at their great shorts, their great T-shirts and tennis shoes. But after you see 1,000 Americans in their great T-shirts, you're not so enthusiastic. And they had a teaching attitude about everything. After a while their teaching begins to bore you.

But teaching may be the one positive thing the Americans can give the Czechs—teaching them how to run a successful business and be survivors and not victims in the new free-market economy. To do this, the Americans must be willing, however, to give the Czechs the freedom to make their own mistakes and learn from them. Many Czechs now look forward to the day when the Americans will return home. When they do, they will hopefully leave behind a new generation of Czechs who have the experience and confidence to success on their own.

National Security

Having suffered at the hands of Nazi Germany and Soviet Russia for half a century, the Czechs are anxious to avoid foreign domination in the future. The best route to secure their nation and to forge closer ties with the West, they believe, is to become a member of the North Atlantic Treaty Organization (NATO). They are not alone in this desire: Hungary, Poland and Slovakia have all expressed interest in NATO membership. However, the West—and particularly the United States—has been reluctant to grant it. Part of this reluctance stems from an unwillingness to offend the Russians, who feel their own security threatened by the expansion of NATO to their borders.

As a compromise, the U.S. government has offered the Czech Republic and other countries membership in the Partnership for Peace, a kind of junior membership in NATO, that could later lead to full membership. Both the Eastern European countries and Russia have rejected the Partnership for Peace—for different reasons. The Czechs, Poles and others see it as a halfway measure that is too tentative, while the Russians are pushing for their neighbors to join another group, the Organization for Security and Cooperation in Europe, where Russia will be on an equal standing with other nations and not in a subordinate position.

As negotiations continue in this delicate matter between the United States and Russia, the Czech government waits patiently and continues to build bonds of trust with both the West and Russia.

Václav Havel has been among the most eloquent advocates for his country's admission to NATO. In a thoughtful editorial in the *New York Times,* he has reasonably argued his case that "NATO [by admitting these countries] would expand in the most natural way. . . . It would find an answer to the challenge of the present and evolve into a genuinely pan-European security structure." As for making Russia feel more insecure, Havel countered that "Our entry into NATO would not bring the enemy closer to Russia but would bring democracy closer to Russia."

Slovakia

October 28 used to be an important date in Czechoslovakia. It was on that day in 1918 that the new nation was formed and made independent from the Austrian Empire, which had ruled it for three centuries. But in 1993, the holiday had become something of an embarrassment for both Czechs and Slovaks. How do you celebrate a nation that no longer exists? The split between Czechs and Slovaks was peaceful and amicable, but it left a hole in the soul of both people. Unable to work out their differences, they simply walked away from the problem.

Since then, the Slovaks have continued on their downward economic spiral. Unemployment has climbed higher and higher, while progress toward a free economy has been dismal. After a year of independence, only 5 percent of the businesses in the Slovak Republic had privatized. Vladimír Meciar, who returned to power in 1994 after being voted out of office briefly, seems to be leaning toward Russia and away from the West, turning down a loan from the European Bank for Reconstruction and Development in 1995. This may only further aggravate relations between the Slovaks and the Czechs.

Symbolic of the ill-feeling that still exists between Czechs and Slovaks are the 1,200 Slovak children abandoned or orphaned and living in Czech institutions. The children wait in limbo because neither country wants families from the other country to adopt them. Nowhere is the problem more plain than in the northern spa town of Teplice-Sanov near the German border. Prostitutes, many of them displaced Gypsies originally from Slovakia, do business with visiting Germans along a highway that runs between Teplice-Sanov and Germany. When these women become pregnant, they place their babies in the Teplice-Sanov Children's Home.

"The Slovaks don't want the children themselves but they don't want them in Czech families either," said a spokesperson for the Czech Ministry of Social Affairs. "They don't want their children Czechified." An attempt of the Czech government to send some of these children home to institutions in Slovakia met with strong resistance from children's rights groups who would rather see them granted Czech citizenship.

Ethnic Division

It is little wonder that Gypsy children are stigmatized by both Czechs and Slovaks. Although other minorities—Hungarians, Germans, Poles and Romanians—are not beloved by the proud and sanctimonious Czechs, the Gypsies stir up the most hatred among all groups in the Czech Republic.

Ethnic unrest and racism is on the rise in the Czech Republic. The young anarchist in the foreground has the Czech word for destroy *written on his scalp. Later, the anarchists clashed with Fascist skinheads whose hatred of Gypsies has led to numerous attacks on this minority.* (The Bettmann Archives)

Originally from India, these wandering people, who call themselves Romanies, now live in every corner of the world but most predominantly in Eastern Europe. There are 50,000 Gypsies in the Czech Republic and another 350,000 in the Slovak Republic. While most Gypsies are law-abiding citizens, the larcenous behavior of some have prejudiced many Czechs against them all. This ethnic racism was suppressed by the Communists but has reasserted itself since 1989.

"Roughnecks pitched bricks through the glass [of our apartment] the day before yesterday," Romany Maria Tulejovi of Ceská Lípa in northern Bohemia told an American journalist in 1993. "They are getting bolder. The police never hesitate to arrest a Romany, but when we are victims, they do nothing." In May 1990, 200 skinheads and punks attacked Gypsies in Prague. Since then, at least a half-dozen Gypsies have been murdered by right-wing extremists.

"We can't wait for the country to be flooded by crime," said 24-year-old Jan Vik, a leading member of the extremist Republican Party. "At age three, a gypsy will see his drunk father, his prostitute mother, and all we try to do for him will prove in vain."

The enmity toward Gypsies has been extended to a new minority in the Czech Republic—the Vietnamese. During the 1980s, the Communists brought in thousands of Vietnamese students and guest workers under the policy of international socialism. Today, the Vietnamese are resented by many Czechs who see their presence as a bitter reminder of the Communist past. The government has announced that these foreign workers must leave the country by the end of 1995. It has also ordered that Gypsies who have not applied for citizenship by a certain date cannot receive social benefits.

These acts, along with a call for more tolerance from moral leaders like President Havel, will hopefully diffuse this tense situation before it grows worse.

The Environment

As one of the most industrialized countries in Europe, the Czech Republic has some of the continent's worst pollution: Factories spout poisonous fumes into the air; villages dump their waste into rivers and streams, turning them into open sewers and the rich Bohemian forests have fallen victim to acid rain.

President Havel is among the sharpest critics of the way his people treat their environment, as this description of traveling from Germany into the Czech Republic illustrates:

> [In Germany] there are neat, well-kept fields, pathways, and orchards [in which] you can see . . . evidence of human care, based on respect for the soil. On the other side there are extensive fields with crops lying unharvested on the ground, stockpiles of chemicals, unused land, land crisscrossed with tire tracks, neglected pathways, no rows of trees or woodlots.

The effects of pollution are particularly dramatic in Prague. Millions of tourists have left the city a vast wasteland, littered with the new consumer packaging of plastic, tin and Styrofoam. Air pollution is just as bad. With its lack of ring roads, Prague at rush hour becomes one huge traffic jam, with some of the oldest cars in Eastern Europe spewing forth tons of deadly exhaust fumes. Better roads and newer cars are part of a long-term goal that may take decades to fulfill.

One solution to air pollution, however, is already under way. The government is encouraging the building of nuclear power plants, a cleaner source of energy compared to coal and oil. In the next few years, the Czech Republic should draw 40 percent of its energy from nuclear power, reducing the 75 percent it currently draws from coal. Natural gas is another cleaner fuel source that the government is recommending for homeowners.

But these measures, while positive, must be accompanied by changing attitudes. The Czechs must make their environment a priority, something it never was under communism.

The Czechs have been great problem solvers in the past. They have been in the forefront of history in changing and improving society through social reform, the arts, technology and political ideology. The difficult transition from communism to democracy may present them with their greatest challenge yet. Of all the countries in transition in Eastern Europe, the Czechs may be the people best prepared for this challenge. They have known grief and servitude, but they have also known triumph and success.

This particular national spirit, at once restless and rock-steady, is best expressed by President Václav Havel:

> It is no accident that here, in this milieu of unrelenting danger, with the constant need to defend our own identity, the idea that a price must be paid for truth, the idea of truth as a moral value, has such a long tradition. That tradition stretches from . . . Jan Hus, all the way down to modern politicians like Tomás Garrigue Masaryk. . . .
>
> When we think about all this, the shape of our present intellectual and spiritual character starts to appear—the outlines of an existential, social, and cultural potential which is slumbering here and which—if understood and evaluated—can give the spirit, or the idea, of our new state a unique and individual face.

NOTES

pp. 101–102   "The leaders of the Soviet Union . . . " Tim D. Whipple, *After The Velvet Revolution* (London: Freedom House, 1991), pp. 66–67.

p. 103   "We are experiencing cultural shock . . . " *The New York Times*, October 7, 1994.

p. 103   "Our impression was . . . " *The New York Times*, May 9, 1995.

p. 104   "I am of Bohemian extraction . . . " David Halberstam, *The Fifties,* (New York: Villard Books, 1993), p. 167.

p. 104   "We were so astonished . . . " *The New York Times*, November 5, 1994.

p. 105–106   "NATO would expand . . . " *The New York Times*, October 17, 1993.

p. 106   "Our entry into NATO . . . " *The New York Times, October 21, 1993.*

pp. 106–107   "The Slovaks don't want the children . . . "*The New York Times*, May 12, 1995.

p. 108   "Roughnecks pitched bricks . . . " Thomas J. Abercrombie, "Czechoslovakia: The Velvet Divorce," *National Geographic*, September 1993, p. 29.

p. 108   "We can't wait . . . " *The New York Times*, November 17, 1993.

p. 109   "[In Germany] these are neat . . . " Václav Havel, "A Dream for Czechoslovakia," *New York Review of Books*, June 25, 1992, p. 10.

p. 110   "It is no accident . . . " Václav Havel, *Summer Meditation,* (New York: Knopf, 1992), pp. 126–27.

Chronology

c. 500 B.C.	The Czechs and Slovaks settle on the plains of Central Asia and Russia.
c. A.D. 500	Avars from the East drive the Slavic tribes into their present-day homeland.
620	The Slavs defeat the Avars and build permanent settlements.
c. 700	Saints Cyril and Methodius bring Christianity to the Czechs and Slovaks.
800	The tribes join together to form the Great Moravian Empire.
c. 900	The Magyars break up the empire and conquer the Slovaks.
	Legendary Queen Libussa founds the first royal dynasty of the kingdom of Bohemia.
921–928	Bohemian Prince Wenceslas unites Bohemia and Moravia under a single crown.
929	King Wenceslas is assassinated by his brother Boleslav.
1355	Charles IV is crowned Holy Roman Emperor and makes Prague his capital.

1415	Jan Hus, religious reformer, is burned at the stake for heresy.
1415–1436	The Hussite Wars pit anti-Catholic Bohemian nationalists against the Catholic Holy Roman Empire; it ends in an uneasy compromise.
1526	Ferdinand I, Hapsburg ruler, becomes king of Bohemia.
1618	A Czech revolt starts the Thirty Years' War.
1620	A Czech defeat at the Battle of the White Mountain ends Bohemian freedom; Bohemia becomes a part of the Austrian Empire.
1867	The Hapsburgs join with Hungary to form the Austro-Hungarian Empire.
1914	World War I begins; many Czechs and Slovaks refuse to fight for the Austrians.
1916	Tomás Masaryk and Edvard Benes help form the Czechoslovak National Council in Paris.
1918	The republic of Czechoslovakia is formed under the Treaty of Versailles; Tomás Masaryk is named first president.
1935	Edvard Benes becomes president on Masaryk's resignation.
1938	Czechoslovakia cedes the Sudetenland to Nazi Germany; Benes's government flees to London and he sets up a Czech government-in-exile.
1939	Czechoslovakia is invaded by Nazi troops and becomes an occupied country.
1942	The Czech towns of Lidice and Lezahy are destroyed by the Nazis in retaliation for the assassination of Prague's Nazi Governor Reinhold Heydrich.
1945	Czechoslovakia is liberated by the Soviet Red Army at the war's end.
1946	Benes forms a coalition government with the Communists.
1948	Jan Masaryk, foreign minister, dies under mysterious circumstances; Benes resigns and the Communists take over the government.

1953	Purge trials end in the execution of hundreds of Czechs and Slovaks.
1957	Hardliner Antonín Novotný becomes president.

1968

January	Novotný is replaced by Alexander Dubcek, who initiates liberal reforms during "Prague Spring."
August	A Soviet invasion ends Dubcek's reforms.
1969	Dubcek is replaced by Gustáv Husák.
1977	Charter 77, a human rights movement, is founded by a group of writers and intellectuals.
1979	Dissident leader Václav Havel is arrested and sentenced to four and one-half years in prison.
1985	Mikhail Gorbachev becomes the new leader of the Soviet Union and begins far-reaching reforms.
1987	Husák resigns as party leader and is replaced by Milos Jakes.
1988	Ten thousand demonstrators march in Prague on the 20th anniversary of the Soviet invasion.

1989

November	More than 200,000 people march in Prague, the largest political demonstration since Prague Spring; the Communist leadership resigns and is replaced by a new administration led by Bohemian party leader Karel Urbanek.
December	Marián Calfa, last Communist leader of Czechoslovakia, negotiates a transition of power; Václav Havel is unanimously voted the new president by Parliament.

1990

February	President Havel visits the United States and addresses a joint session of Congress.

1992

June

In new elections, the Movement for a Democratic Slovakia gains power in the region and moves towards separation from the Czechs.

July

Václav Klaus, former finance minister, becomes prime minister of the Czech Republic; Vladimír Meciar becomes prime minister of Slovakia; Havel resigns as president in protest against the splitting of Czechoslovakia.

November

The Federal Assembly of Czechoslovakia votes to dissolve the country into two new republics.

1993

January

The Czech Republic and the Slovakia Republic are born.

February

Havel is elected first president of the Czech Republic.

August

Russian president Boris Yeltsin visits Prague and signs a treaty with the new nation.

1994

January

American president Bill Clinton visits Prague.

1995

May

Polish pope John Paul II visits the Czech Republic and Slovakia for the first time since the fall of communism.

Further Reading

Nonfiction Books

Gwertzman, Bernard, and Kaufman, Michael T., editors. *The Collapse of Communism* (New York: Times Books, 1990, paper.) A blow-by-blow chronological account of events in Czechoslovakia and other countries in Eastern Europe during the critical years 1989–90 from the pages of *The New York Times.*

Hampl, Patricia. *A Romantic Education* (Boston: Houghton Mifflin, 1981.) Czech-American writer gives a warm and thoughtful account of her travels in Czechoslovakia.

Havel, Václav. *Disturbing the Peace: A Conversation with Karel Hvezdala.* (New York: Knopf, 1990.) A book-length interview conducted in 1986 between a Czech journalist and his country's then-leading dissident.

———. *Open Letters: Selected Writings 1965–1990.* (New York: Knopf, 1990.) Previously uncollected essays and letters spanning 25 years, including Havel's famous "Open Letter" to Communist leader Gustáv Husák written in 1975.

———. *Summer Meditations.* (New York: Knopf, 1992.) Havel's first book of essays on politics and morality written since he became president of Czechoslovakia.

Knowlton, Mary Lee, and Wright, David K. *Czechoslovakia* (Milwaukee: Gareth Stevens, 1988.) A fairly comprehensive, if somewhat outdated,

115

introduction for young adults to the Czech and Slovak peoples and their lands.

Littell, Robert. *The Czech Black Book.* (New York: Praeger, 1969.) A gripping moment-to-moment account of the Soviet invasion of August 1968, drawn from newspaper and other eyewitness accounts.

Navazelskis, Ina. *Alexander Dubcek.* (New York: Chelsea House, 1990.) An excellent, well-illustrated introduction for young adults to the life and times of one of Czechoslovakia's most important modern leaders.

Popescu, Julian. *Let's Visit Czechoslovakia.* (London: Burke Publishing, 1983.) Another young adult survey of the people and land that unfortunately contains much outdated information.

Stokes, Gale. *The Walls Came Tumbling Down: The Collapse of Communism in Eastern Europe.* (New York: Oxford University Press, 1993.) A detailed but readable account of communism's fall and its aftermath in several countries, including Czechoslovakia.

Whipple, Tim D. *After the Velvet Revolution: Václav Havel and the New Leaders of Czechoslovakia Speak Out.* (New York: Freedom House, 1991.) A collection of revealing speeches, articles and interviews with Havel, Klaus and other political figures in Czechoslovakia before the country split in two.

Fiction and Plays

Capek, Karel. *Absolute at Large* (Westport, Conn.: Hyperion Press, 1989.) A classic of science fiction by one Czechoslovakia's most imaginative writers.

Cather, Willa. *My Antonia* (Boston: Houghton-Mifflin, 1973, paper.) The tale of the daughter of Bohemian immigrants coming of age in Nebraska and written by a leading American novelist who was herself a descendant of ohemian immigrants.

Hasek, Jaroslav. *The Good Soldier Svejk* (New York: Knopf, 1993.) An uproarious satire about war and modern society that follows the misadventures of a Czech dogcatcher drafted into the Austrian Army during World War I.

Havel, Václav. *The Garden Party and Other Plays* (New York: Grove, 1993.) Biting satires of the Communist state by a leading writer of the theater of the absurd and now president of the Czech Republic.

Kafka, Franz. *Metamorphosis and Other Stories.* (New York: Penguin, 1971, paper.) This volume includes some of the most imaginative and disturbing stories written in the 20th century, including the title story of a man who is transformed into an insect.

Index

Entries are filed letter by letter. **Boldface** page numbers indicate main discussion of topic; *italic* numbers indicate illustrations; page numbers followed by *c* indicate chronology; those followed by *m* indicate maps.